THE CHARISMA EDGE

**A How-to Guide for Turning On
Your Leadership Power**

ISBN-10: 146104815X
EAN-13: 9781461048152
LCCN: 2011915935

THE CHARISMA EDGE

A How-to Guide for Turning On Your Leadership Power

Cynthia Burnham

Dedicated to my mother, Phebe Burnham, who taught me to stand up straight.

୵ᗡ

Be not afraid of greatness: Some are born great, some achieve greatness, and some have greatness thrust upon them.

—William Shakespeare, poet and playwright (1564-1616)

The reason we're successful, darling? My overall charisma, of course.

—Freddy Mercury, musician (1946–1991)

We are all worms. But I believe I am a glow-worm.

—Sir Winston Churchill, statesman (1874-1965)

CONTENTS

ACKNOWLEDGEMENTS

How does one acknowledge everyone who has played a part in a book that one writes? All my teachers, mentors, bosses, coworkers, family and friends who encouraged and believed in me? Still, a few people always stand out for the most recent adventure.

First, my most heartfelt thanks to Jan Thompson, who convinced me that I had a topic that most people didn't know about, even though it seemed obvious to me. I also thank Gary and Cathy Hawk, who reminded me of the joy of finding clarity in one's path and who introduced me to Henry DeVries, my astute, encouraging and thoughtful editor, who encouraged me to stay on track throughout the planning and writing process.

I also thank Paul Nichols, my generous and brilliant husband and musical partner, who forgave me my distraction, my crankiness and my frequent unavailability during the last year. He read and commented on all the drafts with wit and wisdom, and the unprejudiced eye of a non-business reader. He has also served as an example of what he and I have called "throw yourself from the bridge" charisma in the world of musical performance, and I have seen that if an idea wouldn't work for him, it often wouldn't work elsewhere, whether in the business world or on-stage.

Finally, I thank my parents. Throughout these pages, I often mention my charismatic stand-up-straight ninety-one-year-old artist mom, Phebe Burnham, but I also thank my late father, Dr. Robert Burnham, who made me believe I could be anything I wanted, but who always thought I'd be a teacher and a writer. And so, to my surprise and delight, I have become both.

INTRODUCTION

The year was 2009, and I was nervous. I was the emergency fill-in lunch speaker for two hundred fifty people at a defense industry symposium on beautiful Coronado Island, near San Diego. Don't get me wrong. I love to teach and am happy speaking. Standing in front of the room was not an issue. The reason I was nervous was because I had never spoken on this topic before: leadership charisma. And the audience I was facing included at least a dozen admirals and generals, far more defense industry C-level and senior executives, and many of my key clients. I kept thinking, "What have I got to tell these experienced leaders? Certainly they, of all people understand how to have a powerful presence."

Let me tell you how I ended up on that stage.

I spent many years in corporate America with companies such as Duracell, Gillette, and PaineWebber. Most of the time, I felt like an outsider. As a woman executive, I was different. I had no female role models, as I was often not simply the only woman in the room, but sometimes the only woman at my level in the company. However, in a way that was a blessing, because

I made it my study to figure out what worked and what didn't. Also, I was fortunate to have mentors who taught me a different perspective on how to succeed as a leader.

I learned several important things: First, being smart and technically competent is absolutely critical, but it isn't enough. To be a great leader, whether a man or woman, you need something more, a spark that makes people want to follow you. Second, I learned that relationships and politics are important, and if you can't connect with people quickly, you'll never build the collaborative network you need to succeed. Third, I learned that a leader is always on stage and most people don't know how to play the part.

Most important, I learned that if you study and listen to your mentors and teachers, you can learn to do all these things. You can get the advantage that spark, connection and performance give you: the charisma edge.

This helped me be very successful, and I ended up as a senior vice president on Wall Street. And, I was working constant eleven-to-fourteen-hour days, taking overseas conference calls in the middle of the night, and working holidays, weekends and vacations. I decided that if I was going to work that hard, I wanted the freedom to run my own business. I also wanted to spend time with my eighty-five-year-old mother who was still in my hometown of San Diego. So in 2005, I quit my job, moved home, and began coaching corporate executives on leadership and communication techniques, which is how I ended up at the defense symposium in February 2009.

To my great surprise, my speech blew the audience away. They didn't, after all, know everything I'd learned. What I thought was simple and obvious was new to them. A CBS war correspondent who had covered the Iraq war said, "Cindy, you've just explained to me why a recent interview of mine worked by accident, and now I will be able to use the techniques on purpose."[1] An admiral said, "I never learned this in my training.

I'm going to behave differently from now on." Most importantly, an executive came up to me and said "Cindy, why aren't you teaching this full time?"

That speech changed my life. Since then, I have been asked to speak many, many times on the topic. I've always loved learning, but I've become obsessed with neuroscience and how it relates to power and charisma, and how we can use our understanding of our natural wiring to change our behavior. I've been able to bring my message to corporate leaders, who need to be real heroes in leading our companies and keeping our economy successful, and helped them take their blinders off and see how they can choose to play that part better and more powerfully. I've made leadership charisma my personal mission. I've become, by accident, a charisma coach. Finally, I found an audience to share the secrets I've learned:

Charisma is a learnable skill.

Charisma is a discipline.

Charisma is a way of managing your focus, your body, your attitude and your voice in such a way that your light holds steady to lead the way forward for yourself and others.

Charisma is easy once you find your own powerful center.

Recently, I got the kind of payoff I look for. I was brought in to work with a corporate leader who had been told he lacked "executive presence." Corporate people rarely use the word *charisma*. They say someone isn't inspiring, lacks impact, doesn't look/act/come across like a leader, or has no executive presence. I call those things charisma. His management told me that they thought it would take him two years to move ahead. But in eight months, he was promoted to president of his division. He told me, "Cindy, I know I owe you an evaluation on the coaching process. Please consider my promotion as your evaluation."

The other payoff? I tell my now ninety-one-year-old mom what I'm doing and get to hear her say, "I'm proud of you!"

THE SIMPLE SECRET

What creates powerful leadership presence? Why do some leaders get ahead, while others who are equally talented fall behind? Why is it some people don't get respect, can't connect and get kicked to the curb despite incredible ideas? This is what I asked myself through many years of struggling to find my way in corporate life. What's the missing ingredient?

Call it charisma. Call it confidence. Call it what you will.

But if you don't have it, you won't get far as a leader.

Everyone has seen a leader who lights up the room when they walk in. People are drawn to them, pay attention to what they say and do, and believe and follow them. They have presence everyone can see, as if they have a power switch turned on high. Their flow of current seems to connect them other people in a way we think of as high voltage or energizing. They are "electrifying."

If you have charisma, you have the edge. You are aligned with who you are at your deepest core and connected with a kind of psychic electricity to those around you. In fact, the bad news is that charisma is so important that some people are able to get by on charisma alone. They succeed while being what people on Wall Street called "all sizzle, no steak," and Texans call "all hat, no cattle." This is generally found out in time. However, if you are able to combine charisma with technical expertise, your trajectory upward will be unassailable, and you will lead effortlessly.

We all have an internal power switch that can make us brighter and more charismatic, more able to connect to the people around us. The problem is that if you are like most people, you chance upon this charisma power switch only by accident, and you never learn to use it properly to give you your best advantage. You may find it intermittently but have no clue about how turn it on consistently. In fact, many people spend their lives with their charisma switch turned completely off, and never reach their full potential. When the stakes are high and the performance level demands quality, instead of switching on their power and cranking up their presence to the highest level, many people retreat into fear, anxiety and nervousness. Their light goes out.

We've all seen careers, companies and ideas that have gone astray because of a leader's inability to make a positive and powerful personal impact. Their lack of charisma makes them vanish like an unlit lamp in a darkened room, and all their brilliant strategies die unseen in the shadows.

The good news is that there's a simple secret to becoming more powerful, confident and charismatic:

The simple secret to being charismatic leader is to look, act and feel like a charismatic person.

Sounds easy, right? And it should be easy, if only you knew exactly what it meant deep inside yourself to look, act and feel charismatic. How does a charismatic leader look, act and feel? Wouldn't it be nice to have a simple instruction guide?

More good news. This book is your instruction guide.

I repeat, being more charismatic is easier than you think, and improving charisma is a learnable skill. It is true that like any skill, some people find being charismatic more automatic and seem to be born to it. An Olympic athlete may start with the advantage of a body type set up for a particular sport. But most people can learn to run, or play tennis, or swim to the best of their own abilities. In the same way, we are all wired to have a free flow of our own best charismatic energy through our systems. All you have to do is get out of your own way, which is what these tips are designed to help you do. When you practice the techniques in this book you will become more powerful and charismatic. This is my promise.

There are nine simple "levers" that you can practice and use to lift your charisma: your bearing, your dress, your expressions and gestures, your handshake, your voice, your articulation, your word choice, your mastery over nerves, and your attitude and identity. Specific methods and techniques for becoming more powerful in these areas are outlined week-by-week in the chapters that follow.

Now, you may read the simple secret and be thinking, "Oh, fake it 'til you make it. Big deal." You are correct. It is a very big deal if you treat it seriously. The simple secret is only "fake it 'til you make it" if you think that acting is only about pretending. The best actors have focus, discipline and practiced techniques that allow them to truly embody a role. They dedicate years to honing that ability and understanding the nuances of body, voice, gestures, emotions and attitude that let the true character come forward.

When people hear "Fake it 'til you make it," they mostly think about the faking part, as if it were a game. The simple secret is a dangerous reality. Your physical behaviors and your intellectual thoughts change who you are for real. There is no pretending or faking about it. Your conscious and unconscious choices change your natural body-mind wiring and your neurological programming. Your surface behaviors seep down into the center of who you are and become ingrained into your personality. Actors know it is sometimes hard to shake a role once learned. Charisma is not about pretending to be someone else. Charisma is about having the discipline, focus and awareness to choose positive, dynamic behaviors that allow a clear path to your best self, so that your own finest character naturally comes forward.

Fortunately, you get to choose. This book is a how-to book containing 101 simple tips to look at in nine weeks and a day to help you find and understand your dynamic center and make the charismatic choice. You learn to flip that charisma power switch to the on position. Follow and practice the ideas in this book and you keep that switch in easy reach. You gain access to your own personal charisma, based on who you are at your deepest, most authentic core. Your true charisma gives you an edge in your life and your work, so that leadership, focus and the ability to touch the hearts and minds of others are always at your fingertips.

We stumble in the dark because we don't turn on the light of our own power and let it guide us. Now is the time to flip that switch.

HOW TO USE THIS BOOK

First, a warning. There are a lot of tips in this book (101 of them, to be exact, not counting extra credit exercises). When I was writing this book, a wonderful colleague read an early draft said, "Oh my gosh, Cindy, I've been reading these tips. How can I ever possibly do all of these things?" I asked him if I should cut some of the tips out. He said, "No! Sometimes I read books I think are padded, where the authors put in fluff to fill them out, but all your content is useful. But how can people make all these changes?"

The good news for my colleague and for you is this: You don't have to do everything all at once. Better yet, you don't have to do everything ever. Every tip you master adds to your charisma and helps you become more connected to the source of your power. This is true even if you only work on a few tips, and even if they are small. Attempting to swallow this book whole is a bad idea, like trying to go through a workbook all in one sitting. If you've ever tried doing that, you'll know how non-productive it is. Instead, learn then practice. Practice some more, then learn something else. As with any successful change, learning about becoming charismatic in bite-sized chunks is the wiser way to go.

You are not just allowed, you are strongly and fervently encouraged to narrow your concentration to one, or two or a few tips at a time. Even a few tips, practiced well, will change your trajectory.

If you have met me, you know that I am a joyful person with a serious commitment to learning. I believe in making it easy to find a path to change, which is why I've adopted a practical tips format. I have structured the information about the nine levers of charisma you will practice into three parts— how to *LOOK, ACT* and *FEEL* like a charismatic person. Each part has weeklong subsections, one for each of the nine levers, to help you focus your energy. I have simplified the areas to make them immediately usable.

Find the tips that seem fun, interesting, or provide you with the greatest leverage for change, and start there. You'll most likely know which ones you'll benefit from the most. Go back later, and do more if you want. You can even make a plan to do them all.

NINE WEEKS AND A DAY TO CHARISMA

I suggest you set a goal of nine weeks plus one day to greater charisma. You may decide to stretch this over a longer period, skip parts, or even stay in one area for an extended time. Whatever works is the thing you should do.

Day One

Read the short introductory section on the body-mind connection, which discusses the underlying power concepts, created by your natural wiring system.

Take the survey to evaluate your own charisma level.

Do the two easy day-one exercises, the Charisma Master Switch, and the B.R.I.T.E.-On Model.

Weeks One Through Nine

Move forward through the three main sections of the book (*LOOK, ACT* and *FEEL*) week by week as outlined below. Keep in mind these are merely guidelines. For example, if you're not done after a week, feel free to stay where you are and spend more time, or move on and come back later. You can even skip around, skip sections, or start first where you believe the best leverage is for you. Do as many or as few as you feel suit you.

Weeks One and Two: How To **LOOK** Like A Charismatic Person
        Charismatic Posture—Amping Up Your Bearing
        Charismatic Pants, Pearls and Piercings—Shedding Light
        On Your Tribal Rules

Weeks Three to Seven: How To **ACT** Like A Charismatic Person
        Charismatic Positions—Lighting Up Your Expressions
        and Gestures
        Charismatic Pairing—Connecting With Your
        Handshake
        Charismatic Pitch—Turning on Your Voice
        Charismatic Pronunciation—Clarifying Your
        Articulation
        Charismatic Prose—Spotlighting Your Choice of
        Words

Weeks Eight and Nine: How To **FEEL** Like A Charismatic Person
        Charismatic Poise—Mastering Your Adrenaline and
        Nerves
        Charismatic Person—Connecting to Your Attitude and
        Identity

There are tips in each of the nine leverage areas that are practical, straightforward and mostly easy. Some sections have additional exercises called Extra Credit Switch Flipper exercises, which give you extra ways to practice.

Weekly Process

As you come to each weeklong section, the process is the same:

Play with the tips and exercises for a week or so. Have fun with trying them out and seeing what difference they make for you. Experiment. Keep doing them until they seem normal.

Start easy. Test them out in different situations, but begin in less-critical circumstances. Starting off with your biggest event of the year could be risky.

Ask for feedback and coaching from people you trust. Ask for advice or impressions, or just find people willing to simply ask you if you are working on whatever tip or tips you have chosen.

Check in with yourself daily.

You can even hire a charisma coach to make sure you practice.

Once the tips in one section begin to feel natural, go on to another area, however feels most right to you. And most of all, don't worry about doing every single one, or everything perfectly. Have fun. Sensing your energy grow larger, brighter and cleaner is the best feeling in the world. Enjoy it.

1
DAY ONE
THE BODY-MIND CONNECTION

S omewhere along the line when you were a child or a teenager, perhaps your mother or father, or someone such as a teacher, a coach or a boss, gave you some great tips about charisma and personal presence. They probably told you to stand up straight, smile, look people in the eye, and to hang out with people who were good influences. These are all good tips, and are the fourth, twenty-sixth, twenty-fourth and ninety-fifth tips in the following pages. If you gave it any thought at all, you probably thought you should do these things because they make you look better, and increase your likelihood of meeting people who would support your success, which are both true.

However, another far more powerful reason for following these tips is this: current neuroscientific and biological research has found that if you behave as described in these tips, you will immediately change physically, biochemically, hormonally and neurologically. You will immediately both feel and truly be more charismatic, based on your natural human wiring.

Furthermore, new findings related to your hard-wired empathy circuitry show that your behavior will also immediately change everyone else around you physically, biochemically, hormonally and neurologically.[2]

UNDERLYING POWER CONCEPTS

On the next few pages, you will read about two key scientific findings that will change forever the way you think about the body-mind connection. I call these findings "underlying power concepts," and they are critical to your understanding. These underlying power concepts are hard science, not mysticism, philosophy or ethics, although all those areas tend to agree. Every tip in this book is connected to one or both of these two research-based concepts, which are in turn based on your inescapable, natural, beautifully efficient and miraculous human wiring system.

The underlying power concepts are the wiring diagram for your charisma, the things you must pay attention to if you want to access and use your full power. They also show that those wise advisors in your youth were right.

Concept One: The Mind Believes the Body

When I was growing up in what is known as East County, San Diego, I learned to ride from the father of a friend of mine on one of their horses, Ginger. Ginger was normally a sweet and obedient mare, but sometimes she would get something called "barn fever." If you've ever encountered that, you know what it feels like. The horse decides that now is the time to go home, back to the barn, and is pretty much unstoppable, especially by a young girl outweighed by some eight hundred pounds. When I complained about being unable to control Ginger, my friend's dad told me this: "Cindy," he said, "Never make the mistake of thinking that you really control any horse. The best you can hope for is to trick them into believing you're in charge."

The same is true for the intellectual mind and the body. The first underlying power concept is that physical input from your body drives feeling and conscious thinking. Always. Instinct trumps intellect.[3] Your system believes and gives priority to the messages from your body, and if that "horse" decides to run for the barn, the best you can do is hold on.

You may think your intellectual mind or the conscious "you" is in charge, and you may never have noticed how much your body decides what you feel and do. However, the parts of your brain that manage conscious thinking, logic, and planning are relative newcomers to the art of survival. They are much more recently evolved than the older, preconscious parts of your brain.[4] These newer parts are like the rider on the horse.

The older parts of your brain operate without what is generally thought of as conscious thought. Imagine, for example, that you are standing on the corner of Fifth Avenue and Seventy-Second Street in New York City, calmly walking north across the street from the old trees in Central Park. (If you haven't been there, pick the largest city you have been in.) The light turns green and you prepare to cross the street. Just as you swing your right foot out over the curb, something catches the corner of your eye, and your body leaps backwards as a speeding yellow taxicab comes squealing around the corner, missing you by an eighth of an inch.

Imagine you are standing in your kitchen. A glass ketchup bottle is on the edge of the counter; it tips over and heads for the floor. Without your thinking, your hand shoots out and catches the bottle, averting messy disaster.

In either case, did you decide to jump, or decide to catch the bottle? Or did it just seem to happen?

You cannot think intellectually fast enough to react to these kinds of situations. And since life-or-death situations, especially in the ancient world, were often just this sort of thing, your overall body-mind system still puts its trust in the ancient automatic neurobiological systems that have been busy running the bodies of your earliest ancestors and successfully saving them from danger for a long, long (very long) time. Everything that evolved in you as a flesh-and-blood creature is based on that positive track record, which has allowed the human species to dodge a falling boulder or a leaping saber-toothed tiger without conscious thought. You don't say, "Hmm, should I duck that large cat?" You just move. You react first and your body is filled with various chemicals and action hormones to get you out of the way. Assuming you escape, a few seconds later the input will eventually reach the conscious intellect for you to ponder as a warning for the future. Hormones have already determined much about how you feel. If your body says you are nervous, you will believe it, although you may ask yourself, "Why do I feel this way?"

Try to reason with your body and your body will always win. Anyone who has ever faced stage fright or nerves will tell you that saying, "Come on now, stop being nervous," didn't work. You can't talk yourself out of your immediate reactions, at least not directly. When the adrenaline kicks in, your body is in charge, not your intellectual mind. You can of course talk yourself *into* being nervous by creating a scenario of danger in your mind that your body reacts to. This still puts the body in charge. You can't change the hormones already surging through you by consciously and rationally trying to think them away. Your body is like a horse running for the barn, and your intellectual mind is just holding on until it slows down. Instinct trumps intellect.

However, what you can do is this: you can use your intellectual mind to trick your body, and indirectly change those hormones. Your physical body may start the reaction process, but you can use your intellect to intervene and to mediate what happens next. By deliberately overruling what your body is doing, and choosing how you stand, move, breathe and carry yourself, you will change the chemical and hormonal messages your body sends to your brain, which will loop back and change the way you feel and behave. One study by social psychologist Dr. Amy Cuddy[5] showed that as little as *two minutes* in powerful positions such as some described in this book resulted in significant changes in both testosterone and cortisol, the hormones the govern dominance and stress management, and changed the way people felt about themselves.

Tell your "self" to calm down, and you probably won't. Tell your body to relax your face, your back, your hands, tell it to stand up straight and breathe, and shift your focus to your feet or to your audience, and you almost certainly will find yourself feeling calmer. Stand weak, feel weak, be weak. Stand strong, feel strong, be strong.

The critical lesson. Your conscious mind is wired to believe your body, so you must use your intellect to change the feedback loop. "Fake it 'til you make it" can trick your body into giving you better, more powerful, more charismatic messages.

Concept Two: No Man Is An Island

You may have heard it said that no man is an island, and, with apologies to John Donne,[6] no woman is an island either, nor apparently are monkeys[7] and possibly dogs, dolphins and maybe elephants.[8] The second underlying power concept is this: What you do, and what others do, affects everyone at a basic brain-wiring level.

Have you ever said, or felt, "That person has great energy," or conversely, "That person just gives me the creeps"? New neuroscientific discoveries show that those "vibes" are hard-wired brain reactions that cause you to have a physical response. You have specialized, recently discovered "mirror neurons" in your brain that cause you to sync up with others. These neurons automatically make you feel what others feel and vice versa.[9] Mirror neurons are being called the source of empathy, connection and interpreting the intentions of others.

In your brain, mirror neurons are like your muscle-prompting neurons, except when they fire you don't move, you only feel inside a little as if you did. When you see or hear someone else do something, mirror neurons fire in a way that mirrors what you saw or heard. For example, if you see someone smile, your mirror neurons for smiling fire and for a moment your brain "feels" as if you, yourself, have smiled. Inside your brain, you have "mirrored" what the other person did. Your brain says, "Oh, smiling. I know what smiling feels like. When I smile, I am usually happy and my intentions are good, so the person I am observing is probably happy, and their intentions are probably good." Also, because you have smiled internally for an instant, your body reacts as if you have smiled, and sends positive messages to your intellect, and you feel better, and also feel better about the person who smiled at you.

Mirror neurons explain a lot, even beyond one-on-one empathy. They may help explain mob behavior, TV sports, and harmonized behaviors such as line dancing, marching bands and even synchronized swimming. If you're a sports fan, you watch your favorite football team win on TV and feel your heart pound as if you had played and won.

In addition to the philosophical and poetic truism of "No man is an island," neurological science shows that we are all connected through our brain chemistry and the way we co-create neuronal connections in our brains.

Your actions influence how others feel. Your being confident or nervous or happy makes other people feel the same way. There is an adage: "People may forget what you said, but they'll remember how you made them feel." That is because mirror neurons make you feel and remember with your whole body. This connection between you and others acts in an on-going feedback loop and changes your view of the world. What anyone imagines or experiences changes the growth and connections of neurons in the brain, and interactions between people leave them permanently altered, for better or for worse. Through mirror neurons, you are in a constant state of co-creation of your attitudes, feelings and very self with the people around you. Surrounding yourself with positive influences and being a positive influence yourself is quite literally life-altering.

The critical lesson. You really do change other people by changing yourself. And they change you.

CHARISMA SURVEYS

How charismatic do you believe you are? Take the self-assessment survey below, rating yourself as honestly as you can. You may give the second survey (Charisma Assessment) to other people, to check your self-perception. If you don't know the answer to any question, give yourself a "2."

Charisma Self-Assessment

	Never	Rarely	Some	Usually	Always
I am the focus of immediate positive attention when I come in.	1	2	3	4	5
People remember me.	1	2	3	4	5
I am centered and rock-solid in front of the room or one-on-one.	1	2	3	4	5
People often think I am bigger or taller than I really am.	1	2	3	4	5
I am articulate and easily find the words to convey my message.	1	2	3	4	5
I know what my most important message is.	1	2	3	4	5
I give people a more exciting picture of the world.	1	2	3	4	5
I gesture without fidgeting or distracting movements.	1	2	3	4	5
I allow my passion to come through my words and behaviors.	1	2	3	4	5
I have been told I am inspiring.	1	2	3	4	5
I have a powerful and compelling voice.	1	2	3	4	5
I care about what I talk about.	1	2	3	4	5
I am confident.	1	2	3	4	5
I look people in the eye when speaking and listening.	1	2	3	4	5
When I speak, people quiet down and listen.	1	2	3	4	5
I think of interesting stories and metaphors to illustrate my ideas.	1	2	3	4	5
I give people a sense of larger possibility.	1	2	3	4	5
I have a strong, firm and welcoming handshake.	1	2	3	4	5
My clothes, shoes, accessories, etc. are those of a leader.	1	2	3	4	5

People try to copy the way I dress, move or speak.	1	2	3	4	5
People seem to feel connected to me.	1	2	3	4	5
People think I am interesting & want to hear what I have to say.	1	2	3	4	5
People remain interested throughout my conversations or talks.	1	2	3	4	5
People see me as having authority and power.	1	2	3	4	5
I am sought out for advice and insight.	1	2	3	4	5
I know what my path is and other people know I will follow it.	1	2	3	4	5
I empower people.	1	2	3	4	5
I light up the room.	1	2	3	4	5
TOTAL	+	+	+	+	=

CHARISMA POINT AVERAGE (CPA) = Total divided by 28 ____

SCORING – Total and Charisma Point Average (CPA):

28 – 70 (CPA 1.0 – 2.5): You have not yet found your light. You struggle to be seen and make an impact on those around you.

71 – 90 (CPA 2.54 – 3.21): You stay mostly in the background. You come forward on occasion, but have a ways to go before you are seen to your best advantage.

91 – 111 (CPA 3.25 – 3.96): You see yourself making an average sort of impact. You may be stronger talking about or participating in things you love, and you can "manage the room" if you need to. However you would not be described as generally charismatic.

112 –123 (CPA 4.0 – 4.39): You see yourself as more charismatic than average. Some people definitely find you energizing and exciting, although you may be inconsistent or have areas in need of development.

124–140 (CPA 4.43 – 5.0): Congratulations! You see yourself as charismatic and compelling, and believe people look to you as a leader. Use this guide to make conscious choices about what you are already doing, and to know why it is working.

Charisma Assessment

Please evaluate _____ in the following areas.

(Name) _____

If you don't know the answer to any question, rate the question a "2."

	Never	Rarely	Some	Usually	Always
Is the focus of immediate positive attention when s/he comes in.	1	2	3	4	5
Is memorable.	1	2	3	4	5
Is centered and rock-solid in front of the room or one-on-one.	1	2	3	4	5
Seems bigger or taller than s/he actually is.	1	2	3	4	5
Is articulate & easily finds the words to convey his/her message.	1	2	3	4	5
Clearly knows what his/her most important message is.	1	2	3	4	5
Gives me a more exciting picture of the world.	1	2	3	4	5
Gestures without fidgeting or distracting movements.	1	2	3	4	5
Lets his/her passion to come through his/her words & behaviors.	1	2	3	4	5
Is inspiring.	1	2	3	4	5
Has a powerful and compelling voice.	1	2	3	4	5
Cares what s/he speaks about.	1	2	3	4	5
Is confident.	1	2	3	4	5
Looks me in the eye when speaking and listening.	1	2	3	4	5
Easily causes others to quiet down and listen when s/he speaks.	1	2	3	4	5
Tells interesting stories and metaphors to illustrate ideas.	1	2	3	4	5
Gives me a sense of larger possibility.	1	2	3	4	5
Has a strong, firm and welcoming handshake.	1	2	3	4	5
Has clothes, shoes, accessories, etc. that are those of a leader.	1	2	3	4	5
Is copied by others in the way s/he dresses, moves or speaks.	1	2	3	4	5
Makes me feel connected to him/her.	1	2	3	4	5
Is interesting, and makes me want to hear what s/he has to say.	1	2	3	4	5
Remains interesting throughout his/her conversations or talks.	1	2	3	4	5

Has natural authority and power.	1	2	3	4	5
Is sought out for advice and insight.	1	2	3	4	5
Knows his/her path is and other people know s/he will follow it.	1	2	3	4	5
Makes me feel empowered.	1	2	3	4	5
Lights up the room.	1	2	3	4	5
TOTAL	+	+	+	+	= ____

Additional comments about the charisma of this person, including what s/he does well or could improve:

TWO EXERCISES

Before you start the nine-week program to develop your charisma, spend the first day with the two exercises below. All the recommendations, exercises and tips that follow in the nine weeks are based on the idea that you know how to turn on the master switch of your charisma. As you may or may not yet know how to do that consciously, below are two exercises designed to jump-start your energy.

Exercise One: The Charisma Master Switch

You've heard the descriptions, "David is incredibly energetic," "Lily lights up the stage," "Bob's speech was electrifying." We speak of a "current of excitement" passing through a crowd, or "a bolt out of the blue," or a "light bulb going on," to refer to exciting ideas and thoughts. There is a reason we talk this way. Most of us feel that that deep inside ourselves, energy flows through us and out into the world, and charismatic people seem somehow to have a higher voltage.[10] In fact, charismatic people seem to know how to turn that power on at will to focus their physical and mental energy, like flipping a charisma master switch.

The Dancer. I wish you could have been with me when I saw the dancer. My husband Paul and I were on Maui, at a slack key guitar and Hawaiian dance event when we were ushered to our seats by a slim young Hawaiian man. Dressed in a red polo shirt and khaki pants, he had the sweet, slightly confused expression and awkward body language I have sometimes associated with people with special challenges, although in retrospect perhaps he was just nervous or distracted. People smiled at him indulgently, and one of the other workers seemed to be keeping an eye on him, redirecting him from time to time. When the lights dimmed, our young usher took a seat not too far from us.

As part of the show, friends and relatives of the headliner were invited to participate, some singing or playing the guitar or ukulele, others dancing the hula in long floral dresses or simple casual clothes. The feeling in the room was much more like a family party than a formal event, nevertheless my husband and I were quite surprised when our usher was called up onto the stage. As he shuffled nervously into place, we prepared ourselves to be kind, like parents at a third grade play.

He stood for several moments in the dancers' spot, just to one side of the musicians, and listened to the beginning of the lovely Hawaiian melody. He took a breath, and suddenly he seemed to grow inches taller, becoming older, more muscular and more powerful. Even his clothes looked better. He began to dance, and he was beautiful—graceful, controlled and emotionally communicative, transforming from a possibly limited usher into an amazing, compelling performer. My husband said the young man looked like he should have been some kind of Hawaiian king, wearing an enormous helmet and a feathered cape, the central figure of a beautiful ancient tableau.

This dancer had turned on his switch, and he glowed like a shining light on stage.

Performers, sports figures, politicians, heroes and charismatic leaders know about this switch, although they may not call it by that name. In the classic 1979 movie "All That Jazz," you can watch Roy Schieder, playing the world-renowned dancer, director and choreographer Bob Fosse, dramatically flip on his charisma master switch. His character is seriously compromised by drugs, alcohol, extremes of behavior and illness. However, the show must go on. So he puts eye drops in his red, hung-over eyes, applies his stage make-up then looks in the mirror and cues himself by saying: "It's showtime!" He then goes out to give yet one more world-class performance. That same "showtime" switch is there and turns on in much more positive circumstances when a race starter says, "Get set!" in "On your mark, get set, go!" or when football players huddle with the quarterback, then slap hands before a play. Learning what it feels like to flip on that switch is your first step to becoming charismatic.

You may already have a sense of where this is. The switch will be somewhere in your deepest central core, and turning it on is a clear physical sensation. That said, the location might be different for different people. For example, I am a singer and a speaker, and I imagine my switch is at the middle of my diaphragm, where I breathe. I feel it in my solar plexus, right below my breastbone. Other people have told me that their switch is where their heart is, or at the level of their navel or deeper in the gut. Wherever it is for you, every single recommendation and exercise that follows in this book must start with flipping that charisma switch to the on position.

Finding your charisma switch is like knowing where to put the key in your car's ignition, and your first exercise will be to find your ignition lock.

Your opening exercise is a visualization to help you shape a mindset for success.

Find Your Switch. First, sit up straight in your chair with your arms resting on the arms of the chair or placed loosely in your lap. Close your eyes for a moment and imagine yourself feeling proud, strong and focused. Feel how powerful you are in that moment. Imagine that there is a light switch in the center of your body that is triggered when you are at your finest, that activates the flow of your best dynamic energy and turns on the force of your charisma. Relax and breathe.

Find that switch now. Where is it? Your stomach, your heart, your gut, your brain? See it in your mind's eye. Is it a light switch? A big junction box? A gigantic lever or a small toggle? Perhaps it is just the removal of a barrier to the light, like a hand in front of a candle. Perhaps it is a key going into the ignition.

Now, while imagining the image you have found, turn it to the ON position. Decide to be the most powerful, persuasive, productive person you can be. Decide to leave behind any habits of nervousness, discomfort, or weakness, and be solidly the best, brightest, most illuminating person you can be. Feel how you suddenly are taller, more vigorous and full of life. Feel how you shine. Feel yourself filling with energy and power, and let that energy extend outward around you, touching the space, the objects and the people around you. Know that from now on, you will find that place as easily as the light switch in your favorite room, and you will turn it on before you do anything, any time you want.

Your power is now ON.

Practice the feeling of turning that switch on and off. Practice feeling the power fill you, then letting it relax.

Now let it go for a moment, and look at the second exercise.

Exercise Two: The B.R.I.T.E.-On™ Model

Now that you've found the ON switch, prepare to use it. The B.R.I.T.E.-On model sets the stage. This model changes how you look, act and feel forever. It shows up a number of times throughout this book, so familiarizing yourself with it will be helpful.

The charisma master switch in the first exercise is the "ON" of B.R.I.T.E.-On. However, just as you never turn on the ignition in your car before doing some preparatory actions, you must do five things before you turn on your own switch.

Think of the "B.R.I.T.E" portion as getting into your car. Before you turn on the ignition and begin driving, as a wise driver you do number of things: check the mirrors, adjust your seat, put on your seat belt, put your foot on the brake, look around the car, and then and only then turn on the ignition and pull out.

Before you turn on your charisma switch and begin your performance, as a charismatic person you will also do a number of things: Breathe, Raise your posture, set an Intention, mentally Tell your listeners, and make Eye Contact. Then and only then will you flip **ON** your switch and go on "stage."

No More Bourbon. Helen Baldassare is a petite, charming powerhouse of a performer based in New York City. She has won MAC/Cabaret, Nightlife and other awards, and she was with the original cast of *Nunsense*, among other regional, stock and off-Broadway shows. In addition to being an amazing entertainer, Helen teaches cabaret singing and performance.[11] Cabaret singing is a lot more like speaking to a corporate audience than you might think, as cabaret singers are as much storytellers as they are musicians. Helen has coached many broadcasters, such as Katie Couric, and corporate speakers, as well as aspiring singers. She helps them avoid the vicious wolf of fear, focus on their listeners and commit to a full performance, so that their words, message and emotions can come through to their audience. Helen describes the charisma master switch extremely clearly.

"When I am ready to go on stage," she says, "before I take one step, I take a breath and think to myself, 'I have something important to say.' I walk out on stage, and I find one person, and I think, 'My performance is going to be so incredible that you will put down your drink and not remember to order that second bourbon.'" Only then does Helen turn on that ignition switch and start her engine. Helen's self-talk is a living example which is very close to the B.R.I.T.E.-On charisma master switch described below. As you read the next chapters, remember these five steps:

B: BREATHE. Before your audience can ever see you, stop and take a breath. This applies whether it is an audience of one or many.

R: RAISE Posture. Stand up straight. Find your relaxed center. A raised, proud posture will tell the audience you are ready, and your body will give a message to your brain that you are prepared, safe and powerful.

I: INTENTION. Remember and remind yourself of why you are there: to teach, to connect, to inform, to entertain or to serve. Focus on the importance of your message as it applies to your audience, taking the focus off of yourself.

T: TELL Listeners. Mentally tell them the importance of what you are doing. Connect with them through your intention.

E: EYE Contact. Make eye contact with your listeners. Connect with them through your expression. Send them your hopes, your intentions, and always your thanks for their continued attention.

ON Switch/ON Stage. Then, flip that switch, turn on the ignition, step out and begin.

All of the steps of the B.R.I.T.E.-On model are covered in greater detail throughout the book. This model is your starting point. Think about the B.R.I.T.E.-On model and practice it until you know where to begin. Then it's showtime.

Ladies and gentlemen, start your engines.

2
HOW TO *LOOK* LIKE A CHARISMATIC PERSON

How do you look like a charismatic person?

How you look is clearly important. A common statement is that you only have thirty seconds to make an impression. In fact, people create their preliminary judgment of you within three to five seconds, and then they may spend twenty-five to twenty-seven seconds looking for evidence to prove what they first thought. They don't always notice evidence that disproves it, especially if the original impression is very strong. This means you want to align your physical self before you are seen, giving time for your body to send positive, powerful messages to your brain and ensuring that when someone does see you, you'll make that positive initial impact. You'll also sense the charisma beginning to move through you as you make these changes.

In this section, covering weeks one and two, we look at two key power drivers for *looking* like a charismatic person:

Week One: Charismatic Posture—Amping Up Your Bearing
Week Two: Charismatic Pants, Piercing and Pearls—
             Shedding Light On Your Tribal Rules

WEEK ONE

Charismatic Posture—Amping Up Your Bearing

A good stance and posture reflect a proper state of mind.—Morihei Ueshiba[12]

Be sure to put your feet in the right place, then stand firm.—Abraham Lincoln[13]

In the summer of 1999, New York Mayor Rudy Giuliani was giving a breakfast speech for an industry meeting at Gracie Mansion.[14] This being before 9/11, he had not yet gained the national recognition he would have later on. I had never seen him before (even in a picture), having only recently moved into the city. But he exuded such an aura of competence and charisma that there was no doubt he was in charge. Whatever you might think of his politics, you would agree that he gave off an immediate sense his power, prestige and confidence.

The first thing you would have noticed about Rudy Giuliani was his bearing. As he walked into the room and stood at the podium, his carriage was strong, and his upright, poised stance indicated he was centered. He looked fierce, proud and searingly focused. He was clearly in control, and all eyes were glued on him before he said a single word. He blazed with charisma.

The best place to start looking like a charismatic person is with your bearing, as this is something people notice consciously and unconsciously before you open your mouth, or before they see clearly how you are dressed or whether you're wearing the company tie. Changing how you stand, sit and walk will have the simplest, greatest and easiest impact on your charisma and powerful presence, instantly changing the way you look.

This week, practice turning up your own bearing and your walk to their most powerful volume. Read through the tips and find one or two that you can practice immediately. Work on them throughout the week until they become second nature, and incorporate them into the B.R.I.T.E.-On model that you learned in the Day One exercises. Add additional behaviors only after you are comfortable, and remember that you need not do everything all at once, or even ever. One thing done well is better than ten done badly. Even one new behavior will have an immediate impact on how people perceive you and how you feel within yourself.

I. **Breathe.**
    Inhale. Exhale. In leadership as in life, breathing is the most important thing you can do. Taking a deliberate breath helps you reset and center yourself, and the increased oxygen will make you think more clearly, relax and focus. For this reason, it is the first letter, the "B" in the B.R.I.T.E.-On model. Breathe in slowly, counting as you do. Relax your stomach, and allow it to "pooch" out as you breathe. Let your ribs expand. Hold for a moment, and then exhale slowly with twice the count as your inhalation. (For example, if you breathe in on a four count, then breathe out for eight.) Repeat if necessary, and feel yourself settle in.

2. **Stretch your body before moving.**
    Shake out the kinks and stretch your muscles. Swing your arms around, roll your shoulders, circle your head. Remember that your body gives messages to your intellect all the time. Let your body be loose and prepared for action. And breathe, fully. This will not only get rid of some unresolved tension, it will allow your brain to move into a different mode for a moment or two, thereby resetting your focus and also allowing new ideas to slip in.

3. **Cultivate stillness.**

   Seek your powerful, focused center. Locate that center physically in your body. If you are like most people, you feel it positioned somewhere between just below your navel and your solar plexus, the same place you flip on your power switch. Notice that your center stays strong and still, even when you are flipped on. Focus on that center before you move, and all of your movements, whether they are fast and electric or slow and serene, will come from a centered calmness. When you move, that stillness is like a gyroscope that stays upright no matter which way the rest of you turns.

4. **Stand up straight.**

   Straighten up. Raise your posture to the Mountain pose. See the Extra Credit Switch Flipper exercise "The Mountain" at the end of this section, which gives precise instructions about what "standing up straight" really means. (This is the "R," "Raise Posture," of the B.R.I.T.E.-On model.) Yes, you'll look better, but more important, you'll feel better. Your brain is programmed to believe your body. Instinct always trumps intellect. Always. Your ancient wiring gives precedence to the messages from your body because you can't "think" fast enough to jump out of the way of a rolling boulder, a saber-toothed tiger or even a New York City taxicab. Stand with a weak posture, and your body will tell your brain that you need to be defensive. You will both look and feel weaker. Stand strong and your body will send messages to your brain that you are safe and powerful. You will both look and feel more confident. You'll also be taller, appear five pounds thinner, and your clothes will fit better.

Also, height matters. Size gives you a head start on charisma. In humans, as in many animal species, dominant animals take up more room, either literally or psychologically. A study, quoted in a July 17, 2007, article by Del Jones in *USA Today*, said: "Several studies indicate that taller men are more likely to be successful and that the advantage begins early. A 2005 study in Finland found that baby boys who were taller than average by their first birthday earned more 50 years later. The last U.S. President who was shorter than the average man was 5-foot-7 William McKinley 106 years ago." So raise your posture.

5. **Let 'em hang.**

Let your arms hang relaxed at your sides when you are not gesturing. The openness will indicate to others and to your own limbic brain[15] that you are not afraid, not in danger, and not uncomfortable. Some people find it feels odd at first not to be crossing or moving or blocking with their arms. This is a habit. The more you practice, the less you will get in your own way, and the more comfortable you will become.

6. **Pause before entering a room.**

Stop just outside any room for three to five seconds. Your "showtime" starts before the metaphoric curtain rises. Compose yourself, breathe, raise your posture, set your intention (the "B.R.I." of B.R.I.T.E.-On). Mentally and physically prepare, and then make an entrance. If you're with other people, allow them to go in first. The delay will be polite while allowing you time to gather your energy and flip your leadership switch on. Check and clear your mood. Whatever you are thinking and feeling will "read" as you walk in and influence how you are seen. Think: "I am powerful, strong, and I am glad to be here."

7. **Use fewer steps.**

   Lengthen your stride ever so slightly. Step out deliberately and gracefully. As little as an extra inch will do. A longer stride will make you look and feel more powerful and athletic, and allow you to cover the ground more fluidly. Conversely, small, choppy steps look harried, delicate or childlike (think Geisha).

8. **Slow your pace.**

   Combine a slower pace with your lengthened stride. You will find you can cross the same space in the same amount of time in a more elegant way, while using less energy. A slower, easier stride will make you feel like you have things under control and are moving at just the right speed.

9. **Sit up straight.**

   Keep your upright posture when sitting as well as standing. The "R" in the B.R.I.T.E.-On model is not just for when you're out of your chair. Slumping is inelegant, unattractive, and blocks the free flow of energy through you. You have two bones called the ischial tuberosities, or "sitz"[16] bones, at the base of your pelvic girdle. They are side-by-side and together look like a tipped-over letter "B," each sitz bone like one of the loops, pointing downwards. You will not be surprised to know you sit on your sitz. Whether you sit forward in your chair or back, or even lean to one side, you should be able to feel your sitz bones acting as the pivot point for movement. If you sit up straight and put your hands underneath your posterior, you will find you can feel those bones easily. They should be pointing straight down, which will make your spine align without excessive curving or bending, and you can move forward or back while maintaining your posture, avoiding hunching, drooping or sprawling.

10. Hands out of your lap.

When sitting at a desk or table, keep your hands and forearms on the table whenever possible, or at least no lower than the arms of your chair. The more of you that is hidden by the table, the shorter, smaller and less commanding you appear. Also, putting your hands in your lap, especially if they are clasped, increases the likelihood you will slump, worsening an already poor appearance. Sit close enough in so that your entire forearm is relaxed and flat; you can gesture easily and naturally from that position.

11. Step back (or forward).

Step back or forward slightly to equalize (or exaggerate) height differences. Standing closer to a person who is taller or shorter than you are amplifies and intensifies the perception of difference, making you look up or down at a sharper angle and making it easier for others to compare your heights. Standing back slightly helps equalize the view, and decreases the awkwardness of an encounter.

12. Keep your chin parallel to the floor.

Keep your head straight for the most calm, steady and composed appearance. Tipping your chin up or down can look childish or arrogant, or even flirtatious, depending on whom you are looking at. (Think of a rebellious teenager.) This position also allows your voice to come out the most fully and easily.

13. Focus ahead.

Let your peripheral vision take care of the small details. Look out ahead of you, as you do when you are driving a car. This keeps your head and eyes up, and lets people see that you know where you are going. People respond to physicality as if it were psychological metaphor. If you look down at your feet, you are perceived as shortsighted. If you look out ahead, you are perceived as confident, knowledgeable and strategic, all charismatic traits.

14. Raise your chest.

Lift your sternum and roll your shoulders back slightly to keep your chest from collapsing. This keeps your airflow free, makes you look taller and more energized. Dancers use the model that a string is attached to the center of their sternum, pulling them upward. An exercise: Stand with your feet parallel, about hip distance apart. Bend your knees slightly. Put your hands on your waist, and bend from the waist until you are looking straight down at the floor. Keep your back and elbows straight and flat, so you are making an "L." Take a breath, hold it, and then straighten to standing without changing the position of your chest. Let your arms drop in a relaxed way to your side. Breathe. Notice how much higher your chest is, how much easier it is to breathe.

15. Wear comfortable shoes.

Find shoes you can stand and walk in easily. This should be a no-brainer, and yet many people chose style over function. Pain is distracting. Uncomfortable shoes draw your attention away from the audience and your message; they lessen your ability to stand or walk with power and grace. Comfortable, attractive (well-polished) shoes are always worth the money.

16. Keep your upper body still.

When you stand, keep your shoulders still. Shoulders that wiggle around on a snakey upper body look unsteady and therefore make you look (and feel) unconvincing and tentative. When you walk, imagine that your rib cage is a steady boxcar sliding in an easy way along a level railroad track, without excessive twisting, tipping or rocking. Allow your shoulders, arms and head to simply ride on top of your rib cage. Your arms should move, but gently, without pumping or swinging aggressively. They don't provide any extra propulsion, at least not at walking speed, so swinging them is largely a waste of energy.

17. **Use a mirror.**
Observe your posture and bearing. Be objective. Try out different positions. Stand up straight, cock your hip to one side, move your arms in different ways. Does your slump look powerful? How do your clothes look when you straighten and relax your hands versus cocking your hip to one side and crossing your arms? Give yourself a fig leaf. How does that look? Clasp your hands behind your back. Practice your gestures. What looks fluid and powerful versus floppy, nervous or aggressive? What ways of standing, sitting or moving make you look taller, slimmer, more leaderly?

18. **Watch other leaders.**
Notice who looks graceful, confident and powerful. Observe their body postures and their ways of moving, looking at other people or entering a room. Ask yourself how you differ from them, and try out their style. Does it make you feel more confident?

Extra Credit Switch Flipper Exercise: The Mountain

Figuring out how to appear larger is a useful step in becoming charismatic. Practice being as tall and centered as you can. The "Mountain" pose, similar to the yoga position, or "asana,"[17] of the same name, causes your body to give positive messages to your intellect that you are powerful, calm and in control.

Learn the Pose: Think of yourself as a peaceful warrior poised on top of a mountain. You are still, centered and balanced, but you can nevertheless move in any direction from your current position:

Hips square, forward-facing and even, neither one higher than the other.
Feet facing forward, comfortably placed roughly hip-distance apart.
Knees straight or slightly flexed, not locked backwards. Allow your tailbone to relax.
Hands relaxed, at your side.
Shoulders rolled back, rib cage lifted.
Head centered and upright, with chin parallel to the floor.
Eyes forward, face relaxed.

Standing in this position may seem odd at first. You may feel funny, exposed and as if your hands are heavy or left with nothing to do. This is normal. Before giving up on the warrior on a mountain, first watch someone else take this stance. You'll see that it doesn't look strange. In fact, it looks much better and more powerful than the arms crossed, or fig leaf hand positions that many people take. Some people find it more comfortable to have one foot a little in front of the other, with the toes of the both feet pointed slightly out. Try the basic pose first, then this alternative. The alternative is also fine, as long as it doesn't make you shift your weight to one side and cock your hip.

Learn the Difference: First, stand, and take the pose of a rebellious teenager:

Cock your hip to one side so your weight is on one leg.

Cross your arms across your chest.

Slump down into that pose.

Drop your chin toward your chest and tip your head slightly to one side.

Frown.

Look up under your eyebrows like your parents just said something dumb.

Next, hold this position for a few seconds. Allow your body and mind to "feel" what it's like to be in this weak, defensive pose.

Finally, *slowly* unwind, back to the Mountain pose. Straighten your hips, uncross your arms, and let them fall easily to your side. Lift your chest and chin, smile slightly, and breathe. Consider how you feel now: more powerful, stronger and happier.

WEEK TWO

Charismatic Pants, Pearls and Piercings—Shedding Light On Your Tribal Rules

Know first who you are, then adorn yourself accordingly—Euripides[18]

No change in musical style will survive unless it is accompanied by a change in clothing style.—Frank Zappa[19]

Many years ago at the beginning of my career, I went to work as a salesperson for Gillette Safety Razor, in Los Angeles. I had a large key account there called Thrifty Drug Stores,[20] which sold several million dollars of razor blades and razors every year. One December, I had to do a year-end business review with their buyer, and as it was a very large account, I was to be accompanied by four managers, two from the western regional office and two from Boston headquarters. With each of us that came through the door of the account waiting room, the picture got funnier. One by one, all five of us showed up in nearly identical outfits: navy blue blazer, white or blue shirt, red and blue striped tie, and grey slacks. As the only woman, my variant was a grey skirt. I even had on a little floppy red silk tie. The buyer was greatly amused. It was clearly the Gillette uniform. No one told us what to wear, we just knew. Several years later, I moved to Duracell and found everyone wore suits. I changed my wardrobe accordingly.

In another arena, I've mentioned my mom before. You'd love her, because everyone does. She is ninety-one and an incredible artist, who still paints, sells her work, and enters art shows in which she regularly wins awards.[21] She wears her long white hair in a twist on the back of her head, and for art gallery receptions, she sticks a couple of huge African porcupine quills in it, puts on a dramatic and colorful caftan and a bunch of exotic jewelry. "Honey," she'll say, "People want artists to look like artists."

As people see you more closely, they begin to evaluate whether or not you look like a charismatic person. Your clothes, your hair, your accessories and more are all part of that assessment. Human beings are hard-wired to look for signs of friend or foe, tribe or stranger, weak or powerful. Everything visible—everything—is an indicator of your "tribal affiliation," the group of "friends" that you chose to be associated with, or "foes" you want to be dissociated from. They show where you believe you sit in the hierarchy. Neckties, jewelry, hair, make-up or lack of it, tattoos, shoes, teeth, piercings, amount of skin showing or being covered, and anything else you can think of that people see is instantly evaluated by them. You can go outside the rules, but do so knowingly. Recognize that because of our human threat-assessment wiring, others will notice, if only on a subconscious level, and may regard you as strange, unique, or even dangerous.

Nowadays, there is somewhat more flexibility in rules of business attire than when I was starting out back at Gillette, though artists still dress like artists. Prescribing a single "dress for success"[22] is more difficult. Nevertheless, I still believe every company has a standard look, and its own tribal rules.

I once gave a speech for a client, a major defense contractor in San Diego. The people in the room were denying that there was any particular uniform at their company and insisting that the dress rules were quite broad and flexible. So I asked, "Can you tell whether the people in the elevator work for your company or for the country radio station on the top floor?" They easily agreed they could, but they argued that really we were talking about standard business attire, which was a very broad category. Then I took off my suit jacket and brought out three other jackets, which I modeled one by one. I asked the audience, "If you were picking up a senior executive from your headquarters, could you pick them out from the jackets?" They all agreed that one jacket, my original one, was "correct," one jacket, slightly dressier, was "possible," and the other two were completely out of line, one because the fit was wrong and the other because it had a floral print. They had never realized how much they'd absorbed of the rules of their corporate tribe.

Charisma for leaders is generally consistent with both specific spelled out rules, such as a written dress code, and unconsciously learned corporate rules, such as the navy blue blazers at Gillette. In the defense industry senior executives still wear suits. At an electronic game developer, all the men wear jeans and ironed long-sleeved cowboy shirts. The uniforms differ, but they are still uniforms, appropriate to each company. If you show up in a suit when everyone else is wearing shorts, Hawaiian shirts and flip flops, you will be as inappropriate as if the situation was the other way around. This happened to me when I moved back to San Diego from Wall Street, and went to an extremely casual meeting at a local financial services company. They literally said, "It's Friday! We can't talk to you 'til you take off that suit jacket." Fortunately, they hired me anyway. However, inappropriateness will block or interfere with your charisma, and you will have something to overcome, instead of being aligned with expectations.

This week, consciously notice and know the tribal rules of your own organization. Learn to recognize the standards and preferences are of the group you are working with or representing. Is it red ties, porcupine quills or cowboy shirts?

As before, chose one or two tips that you know you can do easily, and add others when those things become second nature.

19. **Chose clothes and visual markers appropriate to your general tribe.**
    Know what or for whom you are dressing. Every company has an acceptable uniform. In the building with the defense contractor and the radio station, anyone can tell where people in the lobby are going. Make a list: What are the pants, shirts, skirts, suits, shoes, jewelry, markings,

fingernails, tattoos of your tribe? What are things that immediately show you to be part of a different tribe? Who do you see that fits the standards, and who do you see that doesn't? How does this affect how they are treated? See the Extra Credit Switch Flipper exercise "Tribal Inventory" at the end of this chapter for a more detailed process.

20. Be the well-pressed version.

Remember that neatness counts. Unless you are a rock star, in the fashion world or in some tribe where the standard rules don't apply, always chose clean, ironed or professionally pressed clothing. This will always make you appear sharper and more powerful, and people perceive it as attention to detail. Rumpled clothing tends to leave the impression that you are careless or unaware. Imagine a doctor or a trial attorney or a political figure or a company CEO with a wrinkled, stained coat or jacket. (Note that this is true even if you work for a video game company. The top people there may wear much hipper clothing, but most of them wear ironed hipper clothing.) You may also consider that it is a rare company where polishing your shoes is discouraged, and neatness should extend to your footwear as well. Scuffed toes, worn down heels, all look sloppy. You should never be able to guess whether a person drives stick or automatic based on the wear on the back of his or her shoes.

21. Make choices based on who you want to become.

Avoid choices that link you to a group or tribe you eventually plan to leave. Most people tend to dress like their friends, both at home and at work. You want to look right to the people you like, and those people will encourage you by giving you compliments and telling you how great you look. However, this often means dressing like those working where you start instead of those where you want to end up. If you are an administrative assistant or a benefits clerk who wants to become an analyst, dress like the analysts' boss, not like the other admins or clerks. If you are the director of finance who wants to become the CFO, dress like the president of the company. One of the reasons cited for women's lack of progress in the top levels of business is the human tendency of like to hire like.[23] Clothing choices can magnify or minimize differences.

22. As you go higher, chose more generically.

Appeal to a broader audience by dressing more classically. Politicians, for example, dress in a very formal, generic way, so as to appeal to the largest group possible. Consider how strange it seems to see the president of the United States or any other world leader in a bathing suit, even if they are at the beach. Also, the higher you go, the more people are likely to judge the tiniest detail of your hair, necktie or make-up (or lack thereof), so you're better off simplifying, or getting professional advice. Awareness of the rules lets your charisma shine through.

23. Remember the details.

Look for the small elements that signify. In the corporate world, scuffed shoes, too much jewelry, the wrong brand of necktie can all label you as an outsider. In other places, those same items can show you as in the right tribe. People notice. Even if only some of them notice, they may point out the "wrong" detail to others. An example: A woman executive was described as lacking in leadership presence. When asked for further elaboration, three senior men mentioned her toe ring, not her job performance. One of the three mentioned that another person had pointed it out to him, almost as a statement of the toe-ring's noticeability, not the fact that he had failed to notice it. Your reputation is built on the conversations of others. If you want to be successful within a tribe, allow your reputation to be built on your positive attention to detail, not your dissing of the tribal rules.

Extra Credit Switch Flipper Exercise: Tribal Inventory

Imagine what you believe to be the absolute "correct" dress code for your organization or your biggest client or potential client. (This is also a good exercise if you are job seeking.) Create a description of the men or women one level or more up from you, answering questions like these: What do they wear generally? What kinds of shirts, tops, slacks, skirts? Do the men wear ties? If so, what kinds and colors? Suits? What kind? Do they keep the jackets on or take them off? Do they wear jewelry, tattoos, particular hairstyles, and so on?

After you have created this description, watch the people around you of all levels. Keep a tally—tally marks or check marks will do—of how many people you see that conform pretty well to your ideal description. Notice what you think of those that do versus those that don't. Notice where they fall short, or what looks out of place. Consider how it changes their image in the company, and how you might change your own image because of this review.

3
HOW TO *ACT* LIKE A CHARISMATIC PERSON

Obviously, no matter how great your posture, and no matter how clearly aligned your attire, at some point you must begin to take action. You not only need to look like a charismatic person but also to act like one. Over the next five weeks, we'll look at details of how to move charismatically in your expressions and gestures, how to have a charismatic handshake, how to develop and use your voice and articulate your words, and then finally, how to choose more powerful language and ways of speaking that underscore your charisma.

Weeks three through seven look at key power drivers for *acting* like a charismatic person:

Week Three:	Charismatic Positions—Lighting Up Your Expressions and Gestures
Week Four:	Charismatic Pairing—Connecting With Your Handshake
Week Five:	Charismatic Pitch—Turning On Your Voice

Week Six: Charismatic Pronunciation—Clarifying Your Articulation

Week Seven: Charismatic Prose—Spotlighting Your Choice of Words

WEEK THREE

Charismatic Positions–Lighting Up Your Expressions and Gestures

Personality is an unbroken series of successful gestures.—F. Scott Fitzgerald[24]

Charisma is a fancy name given to the knack of giving people your full attention.—Robert Brault[25]

In the mid-1990s, my friend Linda (not her real name) had the opportunity to meet President Bill Clinton during his pre-scandal first term of office. Linda is a staunch Republican and has been since college, when the rest of us were hippies or hippie-wannabes. She was not overwhelmed to be meeting Bill Clinton, the man, however she was thrilled to meet the President of the United States, no matter what his party affiliation. She came back impressed. "Television doesn't do Clinton justice," she said. "In person, he is big, graceful and charismatic. The way he moved, acted and gestured was very compelling. When he shook hands and spoke with me, his eyes never left my face, and I felt as if I were in a powerful beam. He gave me the feeling that for that one second I was the most important person in the room, and that he was really listening to me. When he began to speak, his gestures were forceful, clear, and directed. He held the audience's attention effortlessly. He made us all feel as though we were part of a larger, more important effort. It's no wonder people voted for him." ("Though I still don't like him," she added somewhat regretfully.)

Your expressions and gestures are the beginning of the actions that underscore the impressions you made by looking like a charismatic person. Concentrate on ways to connect with the people around you; at its deepest core, charisma is about connection. The front of the room is not a destination. It is your next starting point. Many times you will see a powerful-appearing person take the attention of the room, and then undermine themselves either with weak, childish body language and gestures, or with overly arrogant and off-putting mannerisms. You may feel that your gestures show "who you really are." Consider instead that by choosing different gestures you show people that "who you really are" is in control, dynamic and worthy of attention.

This week, begin to think about your actions and interactions. How are you connecting with other people? In the Day One section "Concept Two: No Man Is an Island" you read about mirror neurons. (Also see Appendix 2.) Remember the loop of mirror neurons that cause you to sync up with others. Changing the way you act changes how others react to you and also how they feel about themselves. Changing how you act changes the way you feel inside, driving awkwardness on one hand or confidence on the other.

Your gestures, movements and actions matter. Find tips this week you can practice, and watch how changing the way you connect to others changes how connected you feel to them.

24. Maintain eye contact when speaking and listening.

Hold your conversation partner to you with your eyes. There are several tips about eye contact in this section and others, and recall that it is the "E" of the B.R.I.T.E.-On model. Charismatic people make others feel like they are the center of the universe, if only for a moment. Bill Clinton, Rudy Giuliani and others known for their charisma never look away. Maintaining your eye contact while both speaking and listening increases your conversation partner's sense that you are interested, focused and curious about them. And, from a neurological standpoint, maintaining eye contact helps your own focus and makes you stay with the connection.

Note. Appropriate eye contact is culturally determined. In western society, for the most part, the listener maintains eye contact and the speaker is "allowed" to look around. This is not the case in all cultures. Be aware!

25. Hold on one extra beat.

Continue your eye contact ever so slightly longer than you normally would. Do not bore holes in someone with your eyes, simply add a tiny, subtle half-breath of attention. Eye contact links you to your conversation partner, and links them to you, in both directions. You tend to break eye contact when you feel that connection kick in, because it's a little scary. Hold on to the connection for just a few extra milliseconds to strengthen and fortify the bond for both of you.

26. Smile.

Use your full smile and give it as a gift. Consciously show people you are glad to see them, even if you have bad news to give them. Keep your expression from being fake by programming your thoughts: Think, "I am very glad to see this person. This person is interesting. I am happy to be talking to this person." Let the smile come into your heart and your eyes. The smile is one of the best-studied human expressions, and many reports show that a smile sends messages to your brain and create positive endorphin responses telling your mind that you are happy even if your smile is fake. A fake smile held eventually becomes real through the overruling of the mind by the body. Also, a smile creates mirror neuron responses in other people that make them feel happier and more welcoming, at least for a moment.

As a note, there are perhaps two people out of a hundred where less smiling may be in order. A very small number of people smile automatically or out of nervousness, and they may risk being considered inappropriately irreverent or lacking in seriousness, especially in certain environments. The rule of thumb for undersmilers and oversmilers is the same: Give your smile fully or not at all. Don't water down the powerful effect by half smiling or smiling when you don't really mean it.

27. Reduce extraneous nodding.

Nod decisively. Limit how much you nod. In our culture, nodding can mean one of three things: "yes," "I understand," or "you have my encouragement to continue talking." Obviously, from time to time you're going to want to nod. Unfortunately, too many people waggle their heads up and down five or six times for little or no apparent reason. This wiggly movement can undermine your appearance of having a still, powerful center, and frankly make you look like a bobble-head doll. Look around a room next time you are in a big meeting. The most powerful people in a room rarely nod enthusiastically. Instead, they nod once, or perhaps twice, in a powerful, significant way, then go back to stillness. They may also use an "upward nod," where the head tips back once obviously. In regular interactions, the upward nod generally indicates simple recognition or notice, as when you see someone across the street, but is sometimes used by more authoritative people in place of a regular nod to indicate command or control.

28. Use open gestures.

Leave your torso unblocked. Gestures that you hide behind, ones that cause you to block your torso, such as crossing your arms akimbo, or grabbing one elbow, or clasping your hands, or creating a metaphorical fig leaf, are all ways of barricading yourself from other people. These positions often look psychologically defensive. Putting your hands behind your back is only slightly better, as it risks making you look like you are a soldier at "parade rest" and reduces the size of your visible silhouette. There are times when crossed arms might be a sign of thoughtfulness or even relaxation. In that case, be very conscious of maintaining eye contact and an open facial expression.

29. Relax your hands.

Release the tension from your hands when standing, walking and gesturing. Many people unconsciously shift their anxiety into their hands. They stand relaxed, but gesture with tight hands, sharp gestures, or stiff fingers. They clench their fists when walking. Let your fingers relax, and generally be more graceful and flowing in your gestures. If you use strong gestures for emphasis, do so on purpose to make a powerful point, not because your nervousness has migrated into your hands. Shake out your hands out of sight of your audience or before speaking. Put a little string around a finger to remind yourself to simply let go.

30. Use adult gestures (no, not *that* one).

On the other hand, let your gestures be controlled in their relaxation. Loose, flippy-floppy hands and wiggly fingers make you look like an excited teenager. Think grace, and the strong, easy flow of energy from your mind, through your body and smoothly out your fingertips. Make fluid gestures when freedom is called for, sharper ones to indicate decisiveness.

31. **Look to some other model than Tweedledum (or Tweedledee).**[26]

Gesture bigger, and either lower or higher than your solar plexus. Allow your elbows to relax away from your body. Gestures at the level of the solar plexus with your elbows clenched to your side tend to make you look like Tweedledum or Tweedledee and bring unfortunate additional attention to any abdominal roundness. Clasped or tented fingers resting on the top of your stomach are especially good at creating this effect.

32. **Avoid any one-finger point (including, but not solely *that* one).**

If you are pointing out into the audience, point with your full hand. In many cultures, including western culture, pointing at someone is considered extremely rude and aggressive, especially if a shake is added to it. If for some reason you have to point, such as when you are counting, point upwards, never at anyone. Some politicians, who struggle to resist pointing (and shaking their finger) have modified their point to the "pinched point," that is, index and middle finger pinched to the thumb, with ring finger and little finger clenched closed. Some speakers also point with two fingers, the index and middle together. While the full hand is still preferred, this other modifications may be workable, and better than a single finger (of any kind), for those who are burdened by the need to point pointedly.

33. **Save touch for important gestures.**

Touch your heart so show feeling, touch your temple to show thinking, touch your watch to show time, but keep your hands away from your face, hair, jewelry, neck, or any other body part or accessory that is not connected to your message. Touch is important and reassuring to humans, like a mother or father comforting a baby. And we reassure ourselves by touching ourselves if Mom isn't there. Putting your hand on your cheek or mouth, flipping, stroking or twirling your hair (I've seen both men and women do this) grabbing the back of your neck, or other similar gestures make you look like an awkward child. Unfortunately, while those movements may reassure you, they show your listener that you are nervous and uncomfortable. Being visibly nervous and uncomfortable is never charismatic in a leader.

34. Hands out of pockets.

Show your hands. What the heck have you got in there, anyhow? Keeping your hands in your pockets is a clear body-language indicator that you have something to hide. While women have a greater tendency to fiddle with their hair, the more-often-male tendency to jiggle change or keys in pants pockets is equally annoying and not leaderly. It is distracting from a visual standpoint and can also be noisy. Ask yourself where you want your audience's attention: on your face or your pockets.

35. Cock your head like a puppy.

Show you are curious and interested. Tip your head very slightly, and smile when you listen to people. Everyone likes to think they are interesting and worthy of your curiosity. Think of the charm of a puppy when it turns its head to one side. One note: To stay in a powerful pose, maintain your posture upright as you simply drop your ear toward your shoulder. Keep the back-to-front angle of your head fairly perpendicular to the floor, that is, don't tip your face forward or back any more than necessary, and resist slumping. Then, set your chin back to parallel to the floor when you speak.

36. Flash them.

Greet people with a smile, and lift your eyebrows quickly one time. This is called an "eyebrow flash," and it is a body language indicator of interest. Like all messages from the body, using indicators of interest make you feel more genuinely interested and make others connect more to you. Your interest makes others find you charismatic.

37. Watch your feet.

Consciously keep your feet pointed toward your chosen point of interest. If you don't pay attention, your feet automatically point where your heart wants to go, which may not be the message that you want to give as a leader, especially if one foot is pointed toward the door. Putting your feet back in place also resets your own focus back to the present conversation.[27]

WEEK FOUR

Charismatic Pairing—Connecting With Your Handshake

I can feel the twinkle of his eye in his handshake.—Helen Keller[28]

At a conference on business development techniques, one of the speakers was a former Navy Seal I will call John. In front of the room, John was articulate and charming. As one might expect from a member such a prestigious branch of the service, he was also physically imposing, with beautiful posture, an easy, poised-but-energetic demeanor and open, graceful gestures. Afterwards, a woman who was attending along with me went to introduce herself to him and came back with a quizzical look on her face.

"Up close," she said, "he just doesn't seem like a Seal."

I wondered what she meant, so I went and stood in a group waiting to chat with him. I neither saw nor heard anything that made me doubt him. Then I shook his hand. His handshake was not what I would have anticipated from that stern and disciplined background. He had a soft, almost pressure-less grip, as if my hand were a delicate and fragile piece of glass filigree that might break if touched, or less positively, as if he really didn't want to touch my hand. Without exaggeration, it was among the softest handshakes I've ever felt. I watched my own reactions as suddenly he no longer appeared powerful and superior, but instead hesitant and lacking in confidence. I even thought that maybe he was a germaphobe. I experienced this change in my perception despite knowing the power of a handshake to affect a person's response, my conscious realization of what was happening, and my awareness of the personal courage required to be part of the Navy Seals, which includes rigorous physical and mental training that knocks out 85 percent of the applicants.

I don't know if Navy Seals receive training in shaking hands, especially with women. However, this is not to say that they shouldn't. Scientific studies have backed up the importance of handshakes in making a positive first impression. A study by the University of Alabama[29] said: "It would be something of an overstatement to claim that a person's handshake provides a window to his or her soul... [However] Given what we know about the potency of first impressions, it might be a good idea to heed the recommendations of experts on handshaking etiquette and try to make that first handshake a firm one."

The University of Iowa conducted another study related to job applicants and interviewer's first impressions.[30] The authors found, "Quality of handshake was related to interviewer hiring recommendations ... even after controlling for differences in candidate physical appearance and dress."

As an aside, both studies found a suggestion that the relationship between a firm handshake and a positive impression was strong for both sexes but stronger for women.

Your handshake merits a separate focus all its own. The sense of touch is incredibly powerful. In western business society, the handshake is one of the few ways you can touch and connect with another person physically. Many people have no sense of their own handshake and how it may empower or disempower them, even when they have strong feelings about other peoples' handshakes. In the business world, a firm, welcoming handshake will make a connection that little else can, and connection is charismatic. As a note, this is one of the few areas where women have a bit more freedom. An extra touch on the arm, a kiss on the cheek, or even a brief hug is "allowed" even in some of the most formal corporations. Women, use this wisely, in support of your own power, and nevertheless develop a firm, charismatic handshake.

This week, spend your time observing and evaluating handshakes, both yours and those of the people you meet. What works?

What is uncomfortable or unpleasant? What makes you feel like you are making a positive, powerful impression? Review the tips in this section, and practice the B.R.I.T.E.-On model before you extend your hand.

38. "L" your handshake.

Create a powerful, full-coverage link with your hand. Don't minimize this opportunity by only connecting part of your hand. The L of your hand, the angle where your thumb and forefinger meet, should lock into the L of the other person's hand, allowing you a complete grip, palm to palm, with your fingers wrapped around the other person's hand. No half-handed, or worse yet, Queen-of-England[31] fingers-only handshakes.

39. Know your own strength. (Ask.)

Practice your grip and check your strength. Don't assume you know what is right. Ask people if your handshake is too weak or too strong, if you should add force or back off. Find someone who'll allow you to hold the position and change the pressure until you find the right balance of strong but not painful. Also, check with several people, as people do have different preferences. This helps you find a good, medium place where most people are comfortable with your grip.

40. Look them in the eye.

Look at your partner's face before you shake hands with them, not at their nametag, or, worse, at their hand. Put your hand out and let them and your own peripheral vision take charge of the "aim." You won't miss. Hold the eye contact from pre-handshake to post-release, and use your handshake as an opportunity to make a positive impression and connection. You can always look at their nametag a bit later. Focusing on their face will have the added benefit of helping you remember them.

41. Use your pockets constructively.

If you have naturally cold or damp hands, keep your hand in your pocket before shaking hands. A warm, dry hand is more welcoming. Keep a handkerchief (if your hands are extremely damp, a tissue will shred), which also comes in handy if you've just washed your hands. If you have sweaty palms, consider spraying one hand with antiperspirant when you know you are going to have a lot of hand shaking to do. (Roll-on is not recommended, and use talcum powder only if your clothes won't show the dust.) If you have a few moments to spare in a less-visible spot before meeting someone important, rub your palms together and blow on your fingers.

42. Minimize your pain.

Avoid wearing a ring on your right hand, especially if you're doing a lot of hand shaking. If you run across a power bruiser handshake, rings can crunch your fingers. Wincing isn't fun, and looks bad, too. Resist the urge to punish the bruiser by competing in the hard-handshake category.

43. Nothing fancy.

No double handshakes, handshakes with elbow grabs, and so on. Keep it simple. Fancy handshakes can appear overly friendly, overly earnest and inauthentic. This holds for excessive pumping as well, or holding onto someone's hand well after they have loosened their grip. There are few exceptions to this rule. For example, a double handshake might be appropriate for effusive thanks, or possibly when a senior leader gives an award to a junior one. However, a fancy handshake is rarely a good idea, and you are safer keeping to basic tried-and-true.

WEEK FIVE

Charismatic Pitch—Turning On Your Voice

The human voice is the most perfect instrument of all.—Arvo Pärt[32]

The is no index of character so sure as the voice.—Benjamin Disraeli[33]

Karen is one of my favorite people. Up until her recent retirement, she had a high level position with a well-known defense contractor and was actively involved in many industry events and networking functions at which she was frequently called on to speak to hundreds of people. At first blush, Karen does not appear to have obvious advantages for charisma. While attractive, charming and fashionable, she avoids podiums because she is so petite as to be completely lost behind them, even when wearing very high heels, as she often does. Even then, most people tower over her. What Karen does have in spades is a proud and confident demeanor, an ability to remember and greet everyone by name, and a beautiful speaking voice. By varying her tone, pausing and using her pleasing tone to pull people's attention to her, she has a compelling ability to make everything she talks about sound like an interesting story. At a recent event she was at the front of the room doing a general overview introduction of what was to come. As I listened to the sound of her voice, I turned to two younger people at my table.

"I just love Karen," I said.

"Yes," one of them replied. "We think she's a rock star. She makes everyone want to listen to her."

On the other hand, last year I went to a major industry conference attended by eleven thousand people from all over the world. One of the panelists on the morning keynote was an executive from an eighty-thousand-person global company. She was elegant, tall and upright, dressed in a perfectly fitting dark suit, and even from my seat way back in the cavernous hall, she appeared impressive and powerful. However, when she started to speak through the microphone, her voice was extremely unpleasant, nasal and whiney, and her tone had a piercing effect that was magnified because of the amplification system. As I looked around the room, I saw a number of audience members with their fingers in their ears. While it was clear to me that she was successful, I have often wondered how many other of her messages were lost because of people being distracted by the unattractiveness of her voice.

Your speaking voice is critically important. Let your voice support who you are at your best. Have you ever met a woman like my conference speaker who looked terrific, dressed perfectly, had a light-up-the-room smile and a great handshake, and then she opened her mouth and her voice grated on your ears? Or a powerful, physically-imposing man with a high, soft adolescent tone? Suddenly, that wonderful, charismatic, connected first impression goes out the window, and you wince with disappointment and letdown. You avoid listening to what they have to say. But if you are like many people, you underestimate how crucial your own voice is, and how its sound waves vibrate within your own body and the bodies around you. We literally touch each other with the vibrations of our voice. A deep beautiful voice in a man or a woman is as seductive, fascinating and persuasive as physical contact and can transcend almost anything. Your voice alone can have charisma.

When people are physically distant from you, the importance of your voice increases exponentially. This true on the telephone, of course, but also when you are on a large stage, and all people see is a small figure walking around. Even on video or television, any advantage of size or personal magnetism is minimized. Close-ups and talking heads are all the same size. Your charismatic, powerful voice may be all you have to set yourself apart.

Spend this week considering your voice and how you are using it to capture your listeners' attention and help them focus on your message.

An important note: Unless you are a singer or have been taught by a speaking coach, you probably haven't had much practice in this area. You should not be surprised if these tips feel more out-of-character than tips in some of the other areas. Because of this, there are three Extra Credit Switch Flipper vocal exercises included at the end of this section to give you some additional things to work on. For this section in particular, don't worry about changing everything all at once or using every single tip right away. Your voice is a musical instrument, and you will likely need more practice to achieve mastery of it. Also, this is one area where outside coaching[34] or observation can be particularly helpful, and at a minimum you should record yourself whenever possible. Consider buying a relatively inexpensive recording device, or simply use the record functions or applications available on many cameras, phones or computers.

44. Lower your pitch.

Speak from the deeper part of your voice. Lower speaking voices are perceived to be more powerful, more credible, and more pleasant for both men and women. It's a rare voice that is said to be too low. Think of the voice of news broadcasters on radio or TV: men and women both tend to have low, pleasing voices. Mickey Mouse is out, Darth Vader is in. Higher voices in either sex have the tendency to sound harsh, especially when amplified. Hearing your voice at a lower pitch may sound odd to you at first, and yet the depth of your voice is directly related in many peoples' perception to your depth and seriousness as a leader. Check out the Extra Credit Switch Flipper exercise "Finding Your Sea Level."

45. Remove your nose from the equation.

Listen to the tone of your voice. A nasal tone is almost always less attractive. (Willie Nelson is my only real exception.) And if you are a leader, you likely speak through a microphone from time to time, where a nasal whine becomes horrific. Combine it with a high pitch, and people will cover their ears. You can determine the amount of nasality you have currently in your voice by pinching your nostrils lightly closed when you talk. The deeper and less nasal your voice, the less your sound is changed when you hold your nose. The higher and more nasal, the more it will change, sounding very, very "buzzy" when you have your nose closed, with some words practically disappearing. (It will also feel buzzy against your fingers.) Practice until you sound nearly the same pinched or unpinched.

46. Breathe like a sleeping baby.
Breathe in a relaxed way fully into the lower part of your body, not simply high up in your chest. Allow your ribs and belly to expand, and above all, avoid gasping like a fish before you speak. Do the Extra Credit Switch Flipper exercise "Baby Laugh." Practice breathing from this space. It allows your lungs to inflate more fully, giving you more oxygen, clarity and relaxation. Breathe this way when you practice B.R.I.T.E.-On. Notice how it makes you feel calmer and more centered.

47. Start speaking on the breath.
Take a relaxed breath, and begin to speak as you begin to exhale. This is a singers' technique that is also critical in speaking. However, many people start to speak after they've already exhaled for a moment or two, thereby losing air power and forcing themselves to speak in shorter sentences. Alternatively, you may be a person who breathes in deeply, then takes a little mini-gasp of air before you start. Gasping makes you sound rushed, anxious, and

weakens your power. If you find this difficult, practice with sentences that begin with H's or WH's and have lots of round vowels in them, as these sounds naturally propel air. How now brown cow?

48. Open your mouth.

Relax your jaw and speak from an open space. Look in the mirror and watch your mouth as you talk. Does your mouth open in a relaxed way, or do you spread your lips in a stiff smile and speak through a slit? If you cup your hand around your chin, with your fingers on one side and your thumb on the other, can you feel your muscles pooching out? This means two things: first, your voice isn't likely to be relaxed, full and at its most charismatically resonant, and second, you are keeping a lot of the sound inside your own head—a thrill for you, no doubt, but less powerful outside. (Note: Be sure to shut your mouth after you finish speaking.)

49. Open your throat.

Put your fingertips lightly on your larynx (your Adam's apple) and yawn. Feel how your throat opens up and your larynx moves down as you take a breath. Leaving your larynx in the same place, use your Darth Vader voice, and feel how low you can speak. Note how much more sound comes out with both an open throat and an open mouth. Speak in a very high-pitched voice and feel how your larynx shoots up to the top of your throat. Practice speaking with your fingertips on your larynx. Notice when it goes up and down, and work to keep it in a lower position most of the time.

50. Speak forward.

Imagine that your words are coming out through your two upper front teeth. Visualizing this causes you unconsciously to "aim" your air and your voice out your mouth, instead of up inside your own head. Using a low, open mouth/throat voice, listen to how the sound of your voice becomes clearer and less fuzzy as you point it through your teeth instead. Hear how much more dynamic you sound and how the presence of your voice has grown.

51. Use three beans.

Practice relaxing your tongue. (This also helps relax your jaw.) Most of the time, your tongue should be flat and relaxed, like a calm sea, lying loosely behind your bottom teeth. One easy way to practice this at home is with the "three bean" technique. Get some dried, uncooked medium-sized beans. The type is up to you: pinto, kidney, Anasazi, red, even lima beans. (Lentils and split peas are too small.) Wash three of them, so they are clean, and put them underneath the front of your tongue, just behind your teeth. Watching yourself in a mirror, talk for 30 seconds. Focus on keeping your tongue flat, using the sensation of the beans to concentrate your attention. (Avoid swallowing them.) While you do not want to talk to other people with beans in your mouth, the exercise helps you know what it's like to have your tongue in its best starting place.

52. Project using your diaphragm.

Consciously support the movement of your air by controlling your diaphragm. This allows you to speak with more volume, power and control. Your diagram moves up and down under your rib cage. If you put your hand on your belly button and say "ha!" very loudly, you will feel it push the air out quickly. Again, see the Switch Flipper exercise "Baby Laugh." If you gently exhale all your air, you will realize that it is your diaphragm, not your lungs, pushing back and up toward your spine that causes the exhalation to go to its limits.

53. Buy (and use) a cheap kazoo.

Have good time making music on a little plastic horn. It's fun, and a great exercise for your diaphragm, especially as it is quite difficult to make a decent sound on the kazoo without moving air and using your diaphragm. Cheap plastic ones are fine. Blowing up balloons will also show you how out-of-shape your diaphragm may be. If you play any mouth-blown instrument—trombone, piccolo, oboe or bagpipes—practice, and use the same muscles to invigorate your voice.

54. Stretch your voice before speaking.

Learn vocal techniques to loosen up your vocal muscles, your facial muscles, and your lips and tongue. The muscles that move your larynx, or voice box, are tiny, but they are muscles just the same and need to be treated like any other muscle you're going to give a workout. Stretching your vocal muscles lowers the likelihood of vocal strain, hoarseness or soreness. Check out the Switch Flipper exercise "Vocal Warm-Ups," or look for books or lessons on singing for other good ones.[35]

Extra Credit Switch Flipper Exercise: Finding Your Sea Level

Just as sea level is a kind of baseline for measurement, your voice has a kind of "sea level" that offers a baseline of how high or low you should normally speak. Many people regularly speak higher in their vocal register than is most pleasant to listeners. Metaphorically, they speak from a cliff instead of at their natural sea level.[36]

To find your sea level, where you should speak from most of the time, imagine you are about to jump off a cliff into the ocean. It's not a super high cliff, not too dangerous, but just a little exciting. You are going to "jump" three times. Each time you will:

- Imagine taking a deep breath as you run up to the cliff edge, readying yourself for the jump.
- As you metaphorically jump you will shout out loud "AHHHhhhhhhh!" like a downward siren from a high point/pitch of your voice to a low voice.
- You will stop in different places for each of the jumps.

Jump One: Finding sea level. The first time you jump, start high as you lift off, and stop the sound as you "hit" the metaphoric water. Wherever you ended, sound/pitch-wise, say "Ah, Ah, Ah," and notice where that is. Now, staying in that same pitch-place, say, "My name is [fill in the blank]. This is sea-level." It is quite likely you will find this to be lower than you normally speak.

Jump Two: Underwater. Jump again. Shout "AHHHHhhhhhhh!!" again, but this time, don't stop as you hit the water. Allow your voice to take you under the water to its lowest depths, until you feel your toes touch the sand. Now say, "My name is [fill in the blank]. These are my depths."

Jump Three: On the cliff. Prepare yourself to jump. Run toward the cliff and start to shout. But just as you lift-off, stop, as if someone has pulled you back from the edge. Notice where your voice is pitched. From that point in your voice say, "My name is [fill in the blank]. Mickey Mouse has nothing on me!" Notice how this differs from where you regularly speak.

Practice speaking at sea level. Practice dipping down into the underwater parts of your voice. Notice how this makes you sound more serious, and "deeper." Notice when you're up on the cliff, take a breath, and slip down into the cool, safe water.

Extra Credit Switch Flipper Exercise: Baby Laugh

This exercise requires lying on the floor. If you work in an office, you may wish to save it until you are home.

Find and practice the lowest and deepest part of your natural breathing mechanism by lying on your back on the floor with your knees up. Put your hands on your lower stomach, just below your navel. Say, "HA, HA, HA," quickly as if you were laughing loudly, and feel your stomach push the air with each "HA." Now say "HA, HA, HA," with a small, relaxed space in between each sound. Laugh like a baby, and let your mouth stay open. Notice how the breath comes in naturally, on its own, pushing your stomach out and allowing you to be ready for the next exhalation. For even more extra credit, put a book on your stomach below your navel, and see how much you can make it bounce.

Extra Credit Switch Flipper Exercise: Vocal Warm-Ups

These are very basic vocal exercises to warm up your voice. You are more likely to maintain a strong, confident voice, without hoarseness or strain, if you stretch your vocal muscles before you need to speak. Circumstances may not allow you to do these loudly before you speak. You can still practice in your car, do them quietly in the restroom, or even almost silently in the corner of the room.

Hum: Hum up and down a scale, like a humming siren, at a medium volume and speed. Stay in a manageable range, no need to go to the highest or lowest ends of your voice. Do this ten or fifteen times in a row.

High Yawn Sigh: Open your mouth as if you were just about to yawn. In a somewhat soft voice, say "Ahhhhh," starting in at a high very high pitch, and slowly sighing down to the lowest part of your voice. Do this three to five times.

Ning-Ah: Starting in the middle part of your voice, say "Ning," in a very nasal voice, staying on the "Ng" sound, and sliding down into your lower voice, opening to "Ah" as you near the bottom. Make sure your tongue drops flat and your jaw opens on the "Ah" sound. Do this several times, and then do it several more times starting from a slightly higher voice, then higher, until it is no longer comfortable.

Cow Cud and Wow-Wow: With your lips closed, circle your chin around first several times one way, then the other, so you look like cow chewing its cud. Then say "Wow, wow, wow...." a few times, making your mouth as big and open as you can so your cheek and neck muscles are involved. (You can make noise or not, as you prefer.) Then massage your cheeks.

Horse lips: Blow air across your lips so they flutter, like a horse. Or, do the same sort of thing, but make a noise like a motorboat, "brrmmm, brrmmm, brrmmm." This is easier to keep doing if you hold a finger to each cheek as you do it.

Rolled R's: If you can roll your "R's" do so up and down a scale.

Ma-may-me-mo-moo: Say these words on a sung pitch. Raise the pitch slightly and use another consonant (Ba-bay-be-bo-boo). Raise the pitch again, with a different consonant. Go up and down in pitch using different consonants to warm up your lips and tongue.

WEEK SIX

Charismatic Pronunciation—Clarifying Your Articulation

The more articulate one is, the more dangerous words become.—May Sarton[37]

The trouble with talking too fast is that you may say something you haven't thought of yet.—Ann Landers[38]

No word was ever as effective as a rightly timed pause.—Mark Twain[39]

At the Los Angeles campus of UCLA during a brutally hot summer, I was taking extra classes so I could complete my MBA the following March, one quarter early. A class in international economics was held on Tuesday and Thursday afternoons. The subject matter was not one that drew my natural interest, and the timing, from 1:00 to 3:30 p.m., right after lunch, was not one that suited my natural alertness cycle. On top of that, the professor spoke extremely quickly, in a soft monotone with a German accent that was difficult to understand without excellent attention. He never paused as he recited theories, statistics and complex numerical trends. I might have survived all that, but the building was old and there was no air-conditioning. The windows stayed open with the hot air blowing in, and the sounds of the West L.A. traffic made soothing white noise in the background. Unfortunately for me, it was the perfect storm. I would come into the class, and despite multiple cups of coffee, biting my tongue, pinching my leg and other desperate techniques, I would be asleep within minutes, possibly seconds. Ultimately, I had to drop the class. I ended up having to pack twenty units into my final quarter, while working thirty hours a week, and consider myself extremely lucky to have passed all my classes. I have often thought that I almost failed to get my MBA in part because of bad articulation.

Drive your message with well-articulated speech and well-chosen words. How many messages are lost through slurred, boring or inarticulate communication? If you want to be seen as charismatic, every single word you say must matter, and that means clarity and key language choices. This is increasingly important in a world of teleconferences, bad phone connections, aging boomers with hearing destroyed by rock concerts, young people with hearing destroyed by cranked up ear buds, multitasking and all the other assorted ways we miss details in the spoken word. Let the world hear, comprehend and absorb what you have to say.

My perfect storm is obviously an extreme example. However, your audience may be challenged to keep up with you for equally compelling reasons. Clarifying and articulating your words will help them stay with you, and stay alert to what you want them to learn.

This week, pick several tips that shed clearer light your words. Concentrate on pausing or adding consonants. Notice how much more people stay with you when you speak.

55. Slow down. Then slow down some more.

Pause before answering and breathe. Overestimate the time you have. Pausing helps you clear and settle your own thoughts, relax and re-center your voice. Even more importantly, it allows other people to catch up with you and your thinking. You appear and are more thoughtful. An exercise: Spend an entire day pausing two beats before you say anything to anyone. Notice that very few people rush you to be faster, and that your thoughts come up more fully formed, accurate and articulate. Also, pausing gives you time to take a full breath, so that you can purposefully begin, and gives your voice more charismatic power. To help yourself remember, make a small dot with a pen on the back of your hand. Pause each time you see it.

56. Pause three seconds for dignity.[40]

Before you answer any question, count to three. It doesn't matter if the question is hard or easy, important or frivolous. "What do you think of the Yankees' World Series chances this year?" or "Would you accept [a rate three times more than you expected] for that project?" or "Will you marry me?" Pausing three seconds allows you to do three things: confirm your answer is really truth for you, formulate the most articulate response, and show the asker of the question that you have taken them seriously. There is a small additional tip: to look particularly smart, pause three seconds, nod once, look the person straight in the eye, and speak quickly with well-articulated words.

57. End your words.

Put the final consonants back on your words. Most American English speakers drop consonants, especially final consonants. Say this in your normal voice: "Sloppy articulation is neither charismatic nor elegant." If you said it like most Americans, you said something like: "Slobby ardigulashunis neither charismatig nor elegan." Now say: "SloPPy articulatioN is neither charismatiK nor eleganT." You don't have to over-emphasize, though you do have to slow down ever so slightly. Notice how much more precise and powerful you sound when you give the consonants a just a teensy bit more attention.

58. Avoid swallowing letters.

Put the other consonants back. Most regional dialects are interesting, and I never advocate arbitrarily removing any accent. However, in certain regional dialects, consonants get completely swallowed: "miTTen" becomes "mih-en," "roTTen" becomes "rah-in," "cuP oF coffee" becomes "cuh a coffee." "ImporTanT" becomes "impor-in." Not only does this dis-articulate the words, it causes the voice to drop way back in the throat, limiting its resonance and power. From a visual standpoint, this accent also leaves you with your mouth hanging open, which is not good.

59. Separate your words.

Avoid sloppy smashing together of words or syllables. Articulate the separations for effect. Consider "precise and powerful." You can say, "preci sin powerful, " or, "precise | anD | powerful"? Which one conveys the meaning you want? Separations give you more opportunity to pause and allow people to catch up with your thinking and also substantially increase the likelihood of being perceived correctly. After all, if you have a charismatic message, shouldn't your audience hear the right words?

60. Vary your vocal tone and speed.

Pretend you are talking to children whose attention you are trying to capture. How would you tell a story to a child? Add characterization, volume changes, and speed shifts to make a better story. While I am not advocating (necessarily) the use of funny voices, why would you not tell a story with a bit more drama? Do your employees have much greater attention spans than your kids? Does your boss? Put the emotion back into the story. Try out the Extra Credit Switch Flipper exercise "Goldilocks."

61. Sing.

Vocalize loudly and joyfully, in your car, in your shower, in a choir, a karaoke bar, a symphony hall. Sing as dramatically as you can, with excessive emotional emphasis. Play with singing. Singing strengthens your voice, makes you consider volume and intensity choices, and is a whole lot of fun besides. Singing also reminds you of the emotional content of words, since the connection is generally clearer in songs than everyday speech. Think how to bring that intensity to your message.

Extra Credit Switch Flipper Exercise: Goldilocks

Most people know the story of "Goldilocks and the Three Bears," where everything is "too hot, too cold, or just right." When you are looking for drama and vocal variance, you must be all of these things. Most people overestimate the amount of variance in their vocal tone, so this exercise helps you find your upper and lower range.

This exercise works best if you record what you are doing and/or speak in front of a mirror. Try it first with a dramatic text, then with an actual message you might convey in "real life."

Step One: A dramatic text

Find a children's book or other concise, drama-driven story such as a detective, romance, or international spy novel with a lot of action. You might also consider a famous speech, a dramatic play or a poem: "The Highwayman," by Alfred Noyes is a favorite of mine (see Appendix 4).

Read over the text, and mark it: Underline things you want to emphasize. Put parenthesis around things you want to make quiet. Put a line in where you want to pause. Add exclamation points or notes to remind you what you want to stress.

Turn on the recorder, and stand in front of the mirror: Breathe, raise your posture, think of your intention (e.g., "I am going to tell a fabulous story"), tell yourself what you plan to do ("You, mirror image, are going to be mesmerized"), look yourself in the eye, and turn on your showtime charisma master switch.

Read the text aloud two times:
The first time say the text as you normally would. Use the markings you have made on the text, and recite or read as if you were speaking to people you work with.

Then, for the second reading, overact and make the story as dramatic as you possibly can—way, way over the top. Run around the room. Jump up and down. Wave your arms around, and make your eyes big. Change the characters. Think of your audience as non-judgmental children sitting all the way at the back of the room, whose attention you are trying to keep, with a loud, varied, dramatic, interesting voice.

Review the recording: Consider how you sound. Were you more or less dramatic than you thought you were being? Is your sound more or less compelling? How were your voice, your inflection, and your pauses? Consider how much of the behaviors you were using might be translated into your regular speech. If you are like most people, you'll find a lot that is interesting and compelling in what you thought was overacted, or "too hot," and far more that was boring and "too cold," in your normal speaking.

Make a "Just Right" recording: Find the center that captures the energy of the over-the-top exercise, that makes you sound powerful and compelling without being either insane-sounding or boring. Listen to the playback, and adjust.

Step Two: A text from real life
Consider something you plan to say to someone real at a time when you want his or her involvement. Perhaps it is an introduction to what you do at a networking event. Perhaps it is the opening

words of an important speech. Perhaps it is the statement of your vision.

Practice Goldilocks: Go through all the steps you did for the dramatic reading. Record the text as you read it normally, then overacted. Listen, compare and consider how to deliver this kind of message in the future.

WEEK SEVEN

Charismatic Prose—Spotlighting Your Choice of Words

Think twice before you speak, because your words and influence will plant the seed of either success or failure in the mind of another.—Napoleon Hill[41]

Handle them carefully, for words have more power than the atom bomb.— Pearl Strachan Hurd[42]

If you're going to be wrong, be wrong with confidence. And quote statistics.— Dr. Robert Burnham[43]

Gary (not his real name) was a smart, effective leader for his division, a technology developer for major manufacturers. However, at the corporate level, he was described as lacking strategic vision. This was surprising, because if you listened, what he had to say was goal-driven, broad-based, and future-oriented. Admittedly, he was working with strong personalities with short attention spans, but something was awry. Somehow, people weren't paying attention to him. We decided to work on his word choices to attempt to get through to them. We worked out a list of associative, or trigger words, like "broad-based," "long-term," and "high-level" to make people notice he was talking strategy, and he added more excitement words to convey intensity, such as "amazing," or "compelling" or "wonderful" to his normal speech. The next check of his reputation in a formal survey of his peers, direct reports and managers (known as a 360-degree feedback report) suddenly had him described as dynamic and strategic. All he'd really changed was his words. The most interesting outcome, however, was when he said to me, "Cindy, the weird thing is, when I say these words, I feel more dynamic and strategic too." He was rewiring his own brain to become more charismatic.

You may or may not be an actor who easily conveys passionate feeling in your speech. However, you can change your word choices and the ways you choose to structure the information to make them, and you, much more dynamic, powerful and intense. These choices also work to program your own intention to feel like a much more charismatic person and make you vastly more memorable.

This week, use care and thought to consider how the words you choose convey both the meaning you intend and the emotion you want to convey. Remember that the words you use affect you nearly as much as they affect your listener. When you tell a story or chose to describe things in a particular way you program the way your listener remembers and reacts to the facts, but you also program the way you, yourself remember and react. Chose your words wisely.

62. Use trigger words.

Use adjectives that connect to how you would like people to see you or that trigger a stereotype in people's minds. Instead of asking, "What are the implications of this?" ask, "What are the long-term, strategic implications of this?" Instead of saying, "Let's take a broader view of this," say, "Let's look at this from thirty-thousand feet." Some of these expressions are clichés and buzz words, but they work. Other examples include: "Let's look at this from a completely new and different slant," versus "Let's look at this differently." "New neuroscientific research shows that the brain has surprising plasticity" versus "The brain has plasticity." Adjectives add color, and create triggers of association that also help you be more memorable.

63. Use positive language of possibility and motion.

Save "stop" and "don't" for emergencies, such as when someone's hand is over the flame, or a child is about to run into traffic. Talk in terms of what can and should be done, instead of what can't or shouldn't be done. Talk in terms of actions to be taken and priorities to be focused on. Just like a car, it takes less energy to shift direction than to stop and restart, so support people's energy by suggesting they change, shift or even reverse their direction; tell them to do something new, do something differently or modify their approach; tell them to let something go, release a thought, consider what they want to keep from past behaviors and what they want to leave behind. All of this language encourages creative and forward-looking thinking in your listeners, and makes you feel to them like someone who is going someplace they might want to follow. Practice the Extra Credit Switch Flipper exercise "Action Words" at the end of this section for more ideas.

64. Tell a story.

Tell experiences, successes and lessons through stories. Humans are wired to listen to narrative and to tell anecdotes. Which is more unique and memorable: "I help people get promoted successfully," or, "Let me tell you about Rob, who was promoted to head of his function in eight months of working with me, instead of the two years his boss told me he expected"? Throughout history, we have learned ethics and appropriate behaviors from parables, fables and allegories. From "The Boy Who Cried Wolf" to "Who Moved My Cheese?" stories inspire our listeners to pay attention. Interesting stories also create a kind of neuronal node in our brains that makes it easier to remember facts and ideas connected to the story.

Here's one: In 2010, investigators at the University of Missouri, Kansas City, designed a study to determine the effect of scandal on what people remembered about political candidates.[44] The investigators created news stories about fictional political candidates, then tested different groups of readers about what they remembered. One group of readers was given regular news stories about the fictional candidates' political policies and general activities. Another group was given the same stories but with additional stories about a scandal: a lurid extramarital affair that one of the candidates confessed to having had with a junior aide. Both groups of readers were tested for recall at intervals of one to fourteen days later. The researchers had hypothesized that the scandal would be the memorable feature, and would obscure other information about the candidates and the race. Instead, the study found that the group that had received the scandalous stories remembered not only the scandal, but they also remembered the policy positions and activities of the candidates far better than the group who had only been given the non-scandalous stories. The investigators conjectured that a story is an easily remembered kind of node in the brain to which all associated facts tend to stick. If the story is memorable, the facts clustered around are memorable too.

Isn't that more interesting than "stories help you remember?"

This is not to suggest you should create scandals. However, you can, and should, create short, compelling stories which link to points you want to make. Describe what you heard, saw and felt to give details to make your stories live for your listener. Specifics such as names, ages, locations, times of year and dates help people stay in the narrative with you. Check out Extra Credit Switch Flipper exercise "Storytelling."

65. Quote powerful people.

Use others' words for your concepts. In the quotes below, read the ideas first, and notice how relatively simple they are. Then look at the footnotes to see who said these things, and notice how your thoughts shift about the ideas and the quotes.

"Be great in act, as you have been in thought."[1]

"However beautiful the strategy, you should occasionally look at the results."[2]

"If women are expected to do the same work as men, we must teach them the same things."[3]

"An eye for an eye makes the whole world blind."[4]

"In the beginning there was nothing. God said, 'Let there be light!' And there was light. There was still nothing, but you could see it a whole lot better."[5]

Your listeners' brains use other sources as a way to validate both your ideas and your credibility. If another person, especially a prestigious one, said the same thing, it vastly increases the believability of what you have said. Also, quoting someone gives you some of the glow of that person's authority. The more famous, elevated and charismatic the source, the more their fame, elevation and charisma rub off on you. Think how your ears prick up when you hear

---

[1] William Shakespeare, British poet and playwright (1564–1616).

[2] Sir Winston Churchill, British statesman (1874–1965).

[3] Plato, ancient Greek teacher and philosopher (ca. 427 B.C.– 348 B.C.).

[4] Attributed to Indian political leader and philosopher, Mohandas, a.k.a. Mahatma ("Great Soul") Gandhi (1869–1948).

[5] Ellen DeGeneres, American comic (1958–), with apologies to Genesis 1:1.

names like William Shakespeare, John F. Kennedy or Mahatma Gandhi. (Use this technique judiciously. One quote, or two at most, so as not to overdo or look like someone who doesn't have words of their own.)

66. Use specifics and statistics.

Find numbers that support your thinking. People get a sense of believability from "hard" measurements, which shore up otherwise hard-to-accept assertions. Even though most know the quote, "There are lies, damn lies, and statistics,"[45] nevertheless "concrete" equals "true" in the unexamined brain. Your older brain is wired to give preference to hard data versus ideas or concepts, and numbers are about as hard as you can get. Notice how differently you feel when you hear "Oral cancer is a serious problem in America" versus "Every hour of every day, one American dies of oral cancer."[46] You also give statistics strength by personalizing them, especially by connecting them directly to your listener. "Your" brain is more memorable than "the" brain. One "American," or "Bolivian," "Italian" or "Indian," is more memorable than one "person."

One caveat: Statistics are sticky, so make them correct. Even incorrect statistics tend to affix themselves in peoples' minds. Witness the false statement, "We only use 10 percent of our brain at any given time," which has been used to suggest we have excess unused capacity. This has been shown over and over to be wrong and misguided, and yet most people will know that number.[47]

67. Say "Wow!"

Your words show who you are. Use words that convey intensity and show you as a forceful, actively involved and charismatic person. For example, scattering in the occasional adjective such as: interesting, excited, compelling, fascinating, terrific, mesmerizing, captivating, fantastic, riveting, powerful, absorbing, critical, gripping and wonderful shows others that you are involved emotionally in an idea or a subject and helps you share that intensity with others. Think of the difference between "I have evidence," and "I have compelling evidence." Think of the difference between, "I'm glad to be here today because..." and "I'm excited and especially glad to be here today because..."

68. Talk solutions versus problems.

Focus on what you'll do in the future, not what happened in the past. Focus on what you bring forward. Instead of, "We really fouled that up," say, "Here is how we will do things differently from now on." A charismatic, visionary leader looks more at responsibility for fixing something than at blame for causing something. They think about what works, and don't waste energy with a huge concentration on what didn't work, what needs to be left behind or whose fault it was, other than for planning future moves. Talking solutions makes the future nearer, and that is why charismatic leaders often speak of the future in the present sense, as in the famous Martin Luther King speech: "I have a dream..."

69. Remember and use people's names and a detail about them.

Remember at least one thing about a person's story. Remembering their name is the most powerful thing, of course. But even if your forget their name, if you say, "I'm so sorry, I've forgotten your name, but don't you have a Maine coon cat? (live in Marina del Rey, have three children all named Bob, visited Katmandu as a teenager)" they know you were paying attention. Because humans remember stories best, the detail is easier to remember than the name, and remembering it might even trigger you to come up with Duncan McStumblin. One tip to remember names is to clear your mind as you enter a handshake, and remind yourself to remember. If you can attach a mental picture or symbol to the name, especially one that requires your doing something, you substantially increase the likelihood of remembering. For example, imagining patting the person on the cheek when their name is Patty, or trimming their hair if their name is Bob.

70. Make appropriate amends.

If you screw up, or hurt someone unintentionally, apologize. If you've hurt someone but the hurt was unavoidable, say you're sorry that what you did hurt them. Apologizing can make you stronger, not weaker, especially if you explain what you will do differently in the future. A truly powerful and charismatic person is secure enough to survive an apology. Men, though not only men, are particularly prone to apology amnesia.

Or, don't apologize. Don't say you're sorry for things you can't control, didn't do, or are too small to bother with. If you've lost a piece of paper, say, "Hmm, give me a second to find this paper," without saying you're sorry. If someone is standing outside your office door, say, "Gosh, could I ask you to come back in a bit? I'm in the middle of a project," without apologizing first. Women, though not only women, are particularly prone to unnecessary apology.

71. Use the "Rule of Three."

Give three examples, three words, three ideas. In English, listeners respond to the poetic cadence of threes and find groups of three more interesting and easier to remember. "Life, liberty and the pursuit of happiness." "For richer or for poorer, in sickness and in health, until death do us part," "Larry, Moe and Curley." Apparently, more than three is too big, less than three is too small, and three itself is just right. Use sets of three to make your language simpler, more poetic and more memorable.

72. Thank your listener(s).
Always, always thank your listeners before and after you speak, if only mentally. Thank them for their attention, participation, and for allowing you to state your message. Your listeners are your partners in charisma. Having a listener allows you to be charismatic, as charisma is only relevant in context. Connect your thanks to your listeners with eye contact. Allow the gratitude to come forward in your facial expression.

Extra Credit Switch Flipper Exercise: Action Words

Most people are really good at coming up with what they should stop doing. Practice converting negative statements to positive ones. Notice how much more sense of flow and direction come out of the positive actions vs. the negative commands:
Examples:

Negative	Change to Positive
I will stop being so nervous.	I will be relaxed, calm and easy.
I will try not to multitask so much.	I will work to focus on one project at a time.
I will not be so wimpy in meetings.	I will speak out appropriately with force and command.
I will not hide my light under a bushel.	I will_____ _____

I will stop talking so fast.   I will_____.
I will quit my job.   I will_____.

On a piece of paper, make two columns. First write your negatively worded intentions, then convert them to positive.

My DON'Ts (Negative)   Change to My DOs (Positive)

Extra Credit Switch Flipper: Storytelling

Create a story using memorable characters and events to illustrate an important point. Consider the below guidelines, then work to condense it to about two hundred words.

First, decide what is the main point you want to illustrate, such as "stories help you remember," or "bad articulation can make people fall asleep." Think of an event in your life, if you can, that proves or illustrates what you were saying.

Jump in. Do not say, "This is a story about." Begin by describing your starting points. Where did the story take place? A real place, or someplace to be imagined? (If it's not a true story, you must tell your listener to "imagine" or tell them it is a parable or a story, or even a composite.)

When did it happen? Recently? March 2002? The end of summer when you were ten years old? Long ago and far away?

Who was the main character, and what were they doing? What was their name? Is it their real name? What was something about them that was specific and memorable?

What happened?

What is the moral or the conclusion (something about your original idea)?

4
HOW TO *FEEL* LIKE A CHARISMATIC PERSON

B y now, you know how to look like a charismatic person, and how to act like a charismatic person. But what takes it to the deeper level, where you experience the truth of your charisma? How do you *feel* like a charismatic person?

Some of it is obviously from the physical and neural rewiring you have been doing in the last seven weeks, becoming skillful in techniques to change your body behaviors and give more positive and powerful messages to your brain. The last two weeks are spent on two ways to make you feel it: by mastering any remaining nerves and by rethinking your identity into that of a calm, focused, powerful person. These two final areas are in many ways much more difficult that what you have done previously.

In this section, covering weeks eight and nine, we look at key power drivers for *feeling* like a charismatic person:

Week Eight: Charismatic Poise—Mastering Your Adrenaline and Nerves

Week Nine: Charismatic Person—Connecting to Your Attitude and Identity

WEEK EIGHT

Charismatic Poise—Mastering Your Adrenaline and Nerves

He who controls others may be powerful, but he who has mastered himself is mightier still.—Lao Tzu[48]

The essential element in personal magnetism is a consuming sincerity—an overwhelming faith in the importance of the work one has to do.—Bruce Barton[49]

I'm just preparing my impromptu remarks.—Sir Winston Churchill[50]

Many years ago my husband, Paul, a guitarist,[51] read an interview with Andrés Segovia, the late great Spanish classical guitar player often described as the father of the modern classical guitar movement. Maestro Segovia was in his nineties at the time, but still practiced at least two hours a day as he had done throughout his life, even on days when he performed in concert halls around the world.

The interviewer reportedly asked, "Maestro Segovia, you're already the best in the world. Why do you still need to practice?"

Segovia paused, and said without apparent irony, "I intend to be much better before I die."

He knew that the only way to be successful was to work to put his body in charge. By making the physical movements automatic and at the same time learning to be aware of them, Segovia was able to train himself to focus on what was really important, that is, allowing his real passion for the music to come through.

Trick your brain by managing your body. You cannot talk yourself out of being nervous. However, you can often talk your body into revising the messages it's giving your emotional centers, thereby decreasing or slowing the rush of fight, flight or freeze danger hormones. (New thinking has added a third option to the fight-or-flight standard.) Studies have shown that panic attacks, and probably stage fright, are caused at least in part by your emotional centers misinterpreting your body's excitement as danger, since the physical manifestations like pounding heart, shallow breathing and shaking hands are the same.[52] When you feel these things, the best thing to do is ignore the emotion and concentrate on how you can change what your body is doing, or shift your attention somewhere else.[53]

This week, consider the ways you can train your body and focus your mind to support your own passion coming through to those around you.

73. Cultivate stillness (again and always).

Take time every day, as often as you remember, to pause for a moment, breathe and think, "I am still." Add a small hand gesture such as resting your hand on the side of your thigh. The intellectual thought and self-programmed gesture reminds both your body and your mind of what they should do. Then, when you need to, you'll have already developed the habit of stilling yourself down. Mirror neurons (see Appendix 2) cause others to reflect your stillness back to you. You can calm a room full of people by breathing deeply and calming yourself.

74. Focus on your audience and your message.

Have faith in the power of your message. Think about what your listeners will experience or learn that is positive. Before you speak, tell them in your own mind that they are going to love what you have to say. Take the focus off your own nerves and ponder how wonderful and/or important it is for them that you have this message to give them. This the "I,"—Intention—in the B.R.I.T.E.-On model. Not only does it improve your own concentration and give you purpose, it puts your mind where it should be, on your audience and what they will receive.

75. Relax your face.

Let go of the tension held in your face, head and neck. Often people who are otherwise relaxed find the tension has snuck into their faces, in fact, most people hold some tension somewhere in their face, such as their jaw, their tongue, or even their eyebrows. Relaxing your face gives you an immediate sense of center and power while making you look happier and younger. Be specific about your self-instructions. "Relax face: relax lips, relax jaw, relax teeth, relax tongue, relax forehead, relax eyes, relax hair, relax throat, relax back of neck," as many as you need. The more you do this, you find you can begin to shortcut and that your body knows that when you say "relax face," you mean everything that follows, and it will respond.

76. Plant your feet.

Set your feet in a way that gives you balance, and leave them there. Stand steady, and you feel steady. Stand unbalanced, and you feel unbalanced. Your feet should be hip distance apart, toes more or less pointing forward, and either side by side or one foot slightly in front of the other. Feel how your feet steady you. Pull your attention away from your nerves by focusing on the bottoms of your feet. Stimulation from the bottoms of your feet is part of your back-up balance maintaining mechanism (along with your inner ear and the focal point of your eyes). I know of a doctor who recommends the technique of concentrating on the bottoms of your feet to help people afflicted with vertigo. Allowing yourself to feel how your feet connect to the ground translates into a greater sense of psychological balance.

77. Relax your body to disengage your nerves.

Consciously relax your body parts, specifically. As with the face, just saying "relax" is too general. Say instead, "I'm relaxing my hands, I'm relaxing my face, I'm relaxing my tongue, my toes, my knees," and so on. Straighten your stance and hold that position to allow your body and mind to believe it. Your body then begins to give messages to your thinking self that everything is okay, that you are safe, and that you can do whatever you need to do. See the Extra Credit Switch Flipper exercise "In the CEO's Chair."

78. Visualize ahead.

Picture the activity, and picture success, as far in advance of a potentially disorienting experience as possible. Practicing an activity in detail in your mind trains your neurons and your muscles to react appropriately in a real situation. Olympic athletes, Navy Seals, musicians and people about to propose marriage all use this technique to develop familiarity and automatic responses, lower their nervousness and improve their performance. If you feel the slightest nervousness, go back to the beginning and start over after using some body-relaxing techniques.

79. Send goodwill and thanks.

Find an individual and mentally send them thanks, blessings, happiness or connection. Focusing on someone else rather than your own nerves, worries, distractions or boredom brings your attention back to where it should be. A simple, "Thank you for listening," or "I send you hope," or even a mental, "Look how beautiful you are," brings light into your own face, a lowered sense of nervousness, and a greater connection with the people around you. Send blessings. Even if you are not religious, blessings are worthwhile. And make eye contact if you can.

80. Meditate.

Set aside fifteen minutes a day to meditate. Studies have consistently, frequently and clearly shown that a daily meditative practice improves your ability to manage stress, not to mention deal with chronic pain or medical conditions such as migraine headaches. Meditation also improves creativity and general problem solving. There are many, many guides for meditation, some of which are religious and some not. Whatever their source, meditation techniques put your brain in the present moment. Since worry, doubt, regret and stress come from the mind spending all its time in the past or the future, meditation allows you to have a break, which makes your neurons more likely to reconnect in better, more creative ways in the future. See the Extra Credit Switch Flipper exercise "Three Meditations" for some simple ways to start.

81. Exercise, stretch, and sleep.

Keep your body in shape and manage your sleep. Take care of the physical house in which you live. Fit, rested bodies are more able to manage stress. Stretching and exercise also make your body work through and get rid of stress hormones created to help you fight or fly. Like meditation, exercise gives your brain a chance to do something else, which is good for both problem solving and creativity. It also makes you feel and look better, more powerful and often younger.

82. Shake it out.

Shake your hands, feet, or whole body vigorously. Think to yourself that your excess nervous energy is being thrown out your fingertips, like drops of water being reabsorbed by the ocean. Draw one hand down the other arm and sluice the energy off your skin, like you were rinsing water off. Draw you hand over your forehead and the top of your head, and sluice the energy off the back of your head. Create a visual and physical sense of cleaning off that nervousness.

83. Thank your monkey mind and go on.

Acknowledge your inner voice's desire to protect you. All those harassing thoughts ("You're going to screw up!" "What if you fail?" "Remember what happened last time!") are your emotional brain's ways of trying to keep you out of trouble. This is sometimes called your "monkey mind" because of its relation to a concept in Buddhism that says the mind jumps around like a drunken monkey. In some ways, it is more like an overly sensitive smoke alarm than a monkey, warning you with all its loud and annoying might that you could be putting yourself in life-threatening danger, when all you did was burn the toast. Appreciate it. Tell it "I hear you, and I'm going on anyway."[54]

84. Practice (practice, practice).

Rehearse. Visualize. Practice, and practice some more. There is no substitute for training your body and your mind to do things easily and automatically, allowing you to go on consistently even when events conspire to confuse. The best athletes in the world practice their putting, their foul shots, their serves, their batting swings, even after they play. Race car drivers practice avoiding obstacles, watch tapes of their races and walk the upcoming track before they drive. If the best of the best practice, how can you expect to succeed without it? Walk the metaphoric track. Practice to get better and automatic. Practice when it's easy and there's no performance threat. An aside: When people tell me that they think they do fine

"winging it," I always wonder how much better they'd be
if they'd practiced.

Extra Credit Switch Flipper Exercise: Three Meditations

Any meditative practice will help you become more focused,
calmer, and relaxed. Meditation is not difficult, as there is no
real right or wrong way to do it, and sometimes it works well and
other times it doesn't. Over time, it becomes simpler and more
natural.[55] Here are three meditative practices to try:

I. Present Moment Meditation: Sit in a comfortable, upright
position. Your hands can be in any position that feels right:
palms up or down on your thighs, or perhaps simply cupped one
hand on top of the other. You can sit cross-legged on the floor
or on a pillow, or on a chair. If you are on a chair, you will want
to have your feet flat on the ground. Close your eyes and breathe.
On your inhalation, think, *"This."* On your exhalation, think,
"Moment." Repeat. If other thoughts come into your head, notice
without judging or reacting, and go back to your repetitions.

II. Present Moment Walking Meditation: Some people find it
extremely challenging to sit still (those of you who were always
told to "stop fidgeting!" as a child might recognize yourself in that
category). You can also use the present moment meditation, or any
other meditation, in a walking meditation. As you walk, think
about each step you are taking. Think, *"This"* as your right foot
hits the ground, and think, *"Moment"* with your left step. Easy.

III. Smiling Meditation: Your mind believes your body. If you
create a fake smile, your body sends messages to your brain that
everything is okay, and you feel easier and more relaxed. You can
combine this with a general meditation. First, take a comfortable

pose, sitting or lying down, or you can also do this walking. If you are sitting or lying down, close your eyes. Take a deep breath in slowly through your nose, and then expel it quickly through your mouth. Do it one to three times (or more) until you can put your attention and focus into your body. Say to yourself: "I am here now."

Start to smile. Allow a very slight smile to come to your lips. Think, "My lips are smiling." Feel how happy your lips feel. Mindfully, allow the smile and the smile/happy feeling to spread over your face. Notice, "My upper lip is smiling, my chin is smiling, my cheeks are smiling, my nose is smiling, my eyes, eyebrows, forehead, ears, hair, back of head, are smiling." Take a moment to feel your whole head smiling.

Allow the smile bit by bit to spread through your body from your neck (front and back) to your shoulders, arms, hands, chest, and so on, until your whole body is filled with the feeling of smiling. Allow it to spread inside and feel your inner organs smiling, your esophagus, stomach, liver, pancreas, or whatever you remember. Feel the bottoms of your feet smiling. Feel your heart smiling.

Give it away. Imagine the feeling of smiling spreading to everyone or everything you care about. Say "thanks" to whatever Universal source you chose, if any, for the great good luck and happiness you just experienced and gave out.

Take three breaths. Open your eyes if they were closed. Allow your consciousness to return to your body and mind. Notice your relaxation and ease. Stretch, smile, and come back to your regular self with an awareness of how happy you can be.

Extra Credit Switch Flipper Exercise: In the CEO Chair

A study by social psychologist Dr. Amy Cuddy showed that as little as two minutes in powerful positions resulted in significant changes in both testosterone and cortisol, the hormones that govern dominance and stress management, and changed the way people felt about themselves.[56]

You can use the lessons of this study to trick your body into lowering your nervousness and boosting your confidence by spending a few minutes in what I call "the CEO chair" position prior to any stressful meeting or presentation. This position, described below, is one of the most dominant in the western business world. Consider doing this exercise before any event where you think you may feel nervous.

This exercise requires that you be seated at a desk in a chair that can tip back a little. If that configuration is not available, the exercise can also be done in a soft chair or sofa, by a coffee table or ottoman, though at a desk is preferable, because of its height. You can even stand. Feel free to improvise.

The CEO Chair
Sit in the chair.
Interlink your hands behind your head, elbows out.
Tip back comfortably.
Put your feet up on the desk or table.
Cross your ankles.
Relax into the position.

Allow yourself to feel the power of this position. Think, "I'm the CEO of this situation," or even "The king/queen," or any descriptor that you think of as powerful. Revel in this feeling a bit.

Stay in this position for at least a minute, two minutes if you can maintain it. If your arms get tired, you can drop them for a bit, but they should remain in a position that allows your chest to be completely open and exposed, such as stretched out on the back of the couch or chair, or on the arms of the chair with the elbows all the way back. Rock if you feel like it. (If you must rest your arms on your stomach, do not cross them, just clasp your hands loosely). Look out the window, chat on the phone. Notice how you feel more powerful.

Get up out of the chair, slowly, and stand up straight. Notice the rise in your confidence and sense of ease. Take a breath or two, and then go to your adventure.

Warning: This is an extremely dominant position. Be careful when others are in the room. This position is strongly coded, at least in western business situations. On a visceral level, you are saying that you are so confident that you can open up completely and not worry about being attacked. Generally, the posture indicates you think you are the most powerful, "biggest" person in the room. If you are, it is slightly arrogant. If you are not, this position makes you look extremely egotistical.

WEEK NINE

Charismatic Person—Connecting to Your Attitude and Identity

As human beings, our greatness lies not so much in being able to remake the world — that is the myth of the atomic age — as in being able to remake ourselves.—Mohandas Gandhi[57]

Whatever you are, be a good one.—Abraham Lincoln[58]

Olympia Dukakis played the character of Cher's mother, Rose Castorini, an Italian matriarch, in the 1987 romantic comedy *Moonstruck*, which takes place in Brooklyn. In one scene, Rose is sitting in a local restaurant having dinner by herself. A man around her age, a professor played by John Mahoney, is also there having a dinner date with a much younger woman. The man and the young woman fight, she throws a glass of water on him and storms out. Eventually, the professor and Rose have dinner together. He is charmed by her, and subtly suggests they continue involvement in some way. She refuses. When he asks why, she says, "Because I know who I am."

Most of this book focuses on concrete, physical behaviors and actions you can perform to improve your charisma. This week stresses the conceptual underpinnings of charisma, and how your identity, feelings and attitudes come into play.

For better or for worse, charismatic people are clear about who they are, what they want, and what they care about. Clarity and consistency are key. The choices you make about who you believe yourself to be are the ultimate source of how you show up in the world, and most of your beliefs really are choices. There is always another story you can tell yourself that is equally true. For example, you might say, "I had a difficult childhood, which has caused me to have many problems in adulthood." This may be true. A more helpful "story" is: "I am extremely fortunate to

have overcome many of the challenges of a difficult childhood."
This is also likely true, and a more forward-looking statement.[59]
However, the tips about these choices are also the most difficult to
integrate easily. Consider them your life's work, and use the tips in
the rest of the book to underscore, support, and help develop your
charismatic persona. The physical and the attitudinal together
provide a powerful feedback loop to greater presence and charisma.

**This week, and going forward, consider the factors which
influence your personal charismatic identity.**

85. Know what you want.

Spend the time to examine what you really care about.
Define for yourself what message, vision or mission you
represent. Charismatic people are centered on something
they know gives their life meaning. Your drivers might be a
big thing (world peace), or a smaller thing (getting people
to buy into an important task, being a better leader, or
helping other people become charismatic and powerful).
Your drivers may appear different for different parts of
your life, but they generally connect, and whatever your
mission is centers you. You move others best when you
know who you are and what you want.

86. Know what you like.

Know what invigorates you or drains you. Cultivate
clarity of purpose by examining and learning what you're
good at and what you like to do, and conversely, what you
prefer to ask others to do. Notice what you like. This
seems simplistic, and yet it is astounding how many
people focus all the energy on what they don't want or
don't like and forget to focus forward. I have asked many
people what they liked to do in their jobs and been met

by stunned silence. Purposefully knowing, noticing and doing the things that you enjoy, even if you can only do them some of the time, is energizing and uplifting.

87. Have courage.

Be bigger. Step out into it, have the courage to let your energy expand. Taking risks allows your own sense of possibility to grow. Many people are afraid to be as large and successful as they could truly be, for reasons such as fear of failure, outpacing their friends, or looking egotistical. Arthur Samuel Joseph, the great vocal coach says that the two greatest fears are fear of abandonment and fear of owning our power.[60] Be brave and be who you are. Charismatic people are courageous and know they can never be all things to all people. Charismatic people know it is their responsibility to use the gifts they have been given in the fullest possible way. The most charismatic thing you can do is show you are not afraid, or be afraid and show you are willing to move ahead anyway because it is the right thing to do.

88. Stay in service.

Let your mission overpower your fear. Focus on your mission, and keep your attention on the need to bring that into the world. Focusing on your true work takes the attention off you and gives you the nerve to be bigger. Allow people to see that you are in service to something. Whenever you notice, remind yourself of your "job." Focus on it and on being true to that service. When people ask you about what you do, say, "My job on this planet is..." or "My work is..." or "I feel my mission is..." Talk about what you care about to remind yourself as well as inform the people around you.

89. Be consistent.

Let people hear the same message, see the same style and personality every time. Charisma is reinforced by reliability of experience. Repeated behaviors are also easier to remember. Only surprise people by radical changes of appearance or behavior if you plan to surprise them every time and make inconsistency, surprise and eccentricity part of your identity. (We all know quirky artists who are predictably unpredictable.) People are often more disappointed and angered by unmet expectations than by actual behavior. Also, somewhat counter-intuitively, consistently showing others that you are centered on your purpose makes you dangerous and unpredictable in a positive and powerful way, as others know you don't kowtow to the standard, and remain true to who you are despite challenges.

90. Be known for something.

Have a reputation and know what it is. People can generally describe charismatic people in terms of style, dress, message, or behavior; that is how they look, what they do, what they care about. They should be able to say, "Oh, you remember that person. She's the tiny little nun who always wore a blue-and-white habit and fought to help the poorest of the poor in the slums of India." A marketing guru once said, "If you can't be caricatured, you don't have a brand."[61] A similar thing is true for charisma: if you can't be imitated, you don't have charisma.

91. Show delight.

When you are with another person, let your face show you are happy to be there. Think to yourself, "This is a great person," or "I'm glad to have the opportunity to meet this person," or even, "I'm delighted to speak to these folks."

Smile, large or small depending on the circumstances. Even when messages are tough, you can still show respect to individuals by letting them see you take happiness in their presence and that you are glad to be part of their group.

92. Set an intention and remind yourself of it.

Decide what you want to have happen. Voice it in the present and in the positive: "I am a successful speaker," "I light up the room," "Everyone sees me and respects me," "My words are articulate and powerful," "I teach them what they need to know," "My master switch is flipped ON." Say these things to yourself whenever you remember. Make it something you do every time you walk into a room, a meeting, or on stage. *Intention* in its various forms is the "I" of the B.R.I.T.E.-On model. You may be distracted by the details of what you want to do. Bring yourself back to a calm reset position from time to time by looking at the bigger picture of your overall intention.

93. Radiate joy and gratitude.

Be grateful to do the work, whatever it is. Be grateful that it is you being the one to do it. Be thankful for your luck, and allow your joy to come through. Maintaining an inner sense of the supreme luck of being a living person on this planet, at this time, in this universe radiates from you and increases your charisma.

94. Compartmentalize.

Focus on the moment and the job in front of you and give all your energy. Your charisma is like a hose. Just as a hose has more water pressure at the end if you have no leaks along the way, you have more power coming out if you attend fully to one task at a time. Sequence your behaviors versus multitasking them. Many studies have shown that even though you feel like you are efficiently moving multiple things toward completion when you are multitasking, in actuality it takes longer to complete the tasks than if you did them one at a time with full concentration. Remind yourself that you are saving time and increasing effectiveness by centering in. Tell yourself when you will think about the "other" topic later, jot yourself a note if need be, and put it aside. Check out the Extra Credit Switch Flipper exercise "Multitasking" at the end of this section.

95. Gain energy through association with powerful, positive people.

Find charismatic people and spend time with them. Notice which people make you feel energized and elevated, and which people make you feel drained and depressed. Other peoples' energy can absolutely influence how you think and feel.[62] You may not be able to spend all your time with the energy-givers, but maximize your time on the expansive side, and minimize your time on the deflating side. Spend time this week simply observing how other people make you feel. Check in with your gut responses: Do I feel good being around this person or not? How do I feel when I leave? How do I feel when I think about spending time with this person?

96. Ask for feedback.

Ask for help, opinion and evaluation. Be strong enough to ask others how you are doing, generally and specifically. Once they've told you, say thanks without defensiveness. If you don't agree, still say thanks without defensiveness. You can say, "Huh, I never thought of it that way. Thanks, you've given me something to think about." You will be amazed at the wonderful information you get by doing this.

97. **Think about how you might be described and how you'd like to be described.**

Create the image of a new you based on your best self. Consider what your reputation is today, if you have any idea. Imagine two scenarios: first, how people might describe your strengths and shortcomings today. Then imagine how they will describe you in a year, when you've done, or changed, or developed in all the areas you'd like. Think of bringing forward all that you are most proud of and leaving behind what no longer works for you. Create an inner role model for yourself. Give it a name, followed by "ME." You can name it based on a title, a characteristic, or perhaps a role, such as "The Vice President Me," "The World-Class, Powerful Me," or the "Officer Me." Naming your inner role model will give it a place in your brain. Then, act in accordance with what this ideal self would do.

98. **Understand the difference between behavior and personality.**

Reinforce your sense of power by making what is positive a fixed characteristic and what is negative a changeable behavior. "I *am* brilliant, but I sometimes *do* unintelligent things." Define yourself based on your positive, compelling, charismatic traits, and avoid calling something a personality trait when it is really an excuse for your behavior, a personal preference, or even a lack of learning. Are you an emotional person, or do you behave in an inappropriately emotional way? Are you bad at math, or do you not like it? Are you a person who can't sing, or do you simply sing like a ten-year-old because that's when you stopped singing in school? Use "I am" statements to define your positive qualities, such as "I am courageous, charismatic and intelligent." Use descriptions of your actions and what you do to define your negative behaviors, such as "I sometimes behave emotionally," "I didn't figure out that problem," or, "I never studied singing."

99. Say "Up until now."

Couch judgment with an opening for the future. Tell yourself a better story. Instead of "I'm really bad at [fill in the blank]," say, "Up until now I have always been bad at [fill in the blank]." This statement alone helps you recognize the difference between behavior that is changeable in the future and an attribute, which feels much more permanent and locked in. "Up until now, I've been a bad singer," is quite different than "I can't sing."

100. Notice your participation.

Pay attention to what you create, what you support, and what you permit in your life. A mental state full of things you merely tolerate is like a room that you haven't gotten around to cleaning; it's full of dust, debris, old papers, and boxes filled with junk. Working in that room is harder and more frustrating and masks the true issues that may need to be addressed. Just as you may set aside time to clean your office or your house, set aside time to reorder your mental state. See the Extra Credit Switch Flipper exercise "The Reset List of Questions to Ponder."

Notice your emotions as well. Choose what to do about them. Neuroscientist Dr. Jill Bolte Taylor says it takes 90 seconds for an automatic anger response to hijack your body, and then move through if you don't buy into it. By noticing your feelings, you can decide whether to fuel the emotion further or to hold on for a minute or two until the feelings dissipate.[63]

101. Forgive and learn.

Have a generous heart while staying true to who you are. Forgive the doer even while you learn from the deed. Forgiveness of yourself or others allows you to move on and not waste energy on past errors, and teaches you what you want to keep in your life, what to leave behind, and where to find gratitude and joy.

Extra Credit Switch Flipper Exercise: Multitasking

In this exercise, you write the same letters and numbers two different times, but you do it in two different ways, timing how long each takes with a watch, phone or stopwatch that tracks seconds. (Having another person time you can make this easier.)

Both times the page ends up looking something like the below, with the word "multitasking" written in capital letters and a number (1-12) beneath each letter:

```
M  U  L  T  I  T  A  S  K  I  N  G
1  2  3  4  5  6  7  8  9  10 11 12
```

Round One: Time yourself as you write a single letter from the top line then a number from the bottom line, that is, write M then 1, U then 2, L then 3, and so on, going back and forth between the two lines, until you've completed all the letter and numbers.

Round Two: Time yourself as you write out the full word "MULTITASKING," then write out the numbers 1-12 with a number beneath each of the letters.

What does the difference in time tell you? For many people, the first round takes twice as long as the second. Your brain experiences a disconnect-reconnect lag each time you change tasks. While the difference may be less noticeable with small tasks, the neurological lag gets bigger and bigger with larger and more important tasks, and can cause significant delay in order for your brain to reset. If you took twice as long with this little exercise, or even if it took you only slightly longer, consider how much time are you losing during the zillions of switchovers and switchbacks in your day. Compartmentalizing and focusing saves time in the long run and provides more energy for each individual task.

This holds true for focus on people as well. Even in a crowd, focus fully on each person you connect with. Give them your full attention and the full benefit of your charismatic energy.

Extra Credit Switch Flipper Exercise: The Reset List of Questions to Ponder

Questions that you ask about yourself have the tendency to reset your direction. Below are some to ponder. Often, we wait until New Year's Eve to think about our lives or make resolutions. Getting in the habit of asking yourself bigger questions more often makes you a bigger person. (Asking and answering these questions also gives you interesting stories to tell.)

My Past:
What am I most proud of in recent months? In my life?
What have I done extremely well?
What talents and skills do I credit myself with developing?
What happened to me, positive or negative, that I had to react to, or make choices about; how did those choices affect me, and lead me to who I am now?
How have my experiences, positive or negative, contributed to where I am today?
How am I different than I thought I would be? How is my life different? What is better than I expected?

My Present:
What am I most grateful for?
What is most enjoyable in my life?
What do I want to make sure I keep doing?
Where am I focusing right now? Does this feel like the right direction?
What things are right where they should be? (Work, love, family, health, physical, spiritual, financial, etc.)
Have I yet done everything I want to do?
Whom do I love, and who loves me? What do they love about me, and I about them?

My Future:
What do I most hope for?
What do I want to be like going forward? Is it the same or different than now?
What changes of direction, if incorporated now, will make the rest of my life better, more productive, and happier?
If I haven't done all that I want yet, what steps could I take toward those things now?
What do I want to learn, do or see?
Is there anyone I need to contact, visit or forgive?
If I didn't have to please anyone or support anyone, what would I do? Why would that make me happy? What about it is exciting and interesting? Are there any parts of that I could easily incorporate in my life now?
A year from now, what would I want people to say about me?
How would I like to be remembered?
What do I want the rest of my life to be like?

5
CONCLUSION

When I was thirty-nine, during my first stint as an independent consultant based in Norfolk, Connecticut, I was a volunteer for hospice. During the training, we were asked to imagine ourselves in the place of the terminal illness patients we were working with.

"What would you regret," we were told to ask ourselves, "if you were the one lying in the bed and had just been told you had only six months to live? What would you wish you had taken more time to do?"

To my great surprise, the answer that burst through inside my head and heart was not travel I'd missed, or work undone, or family regrets, or even the fact that I do not have children. My regret was: "I always wanted to learn to sing."

That same week, there was a small ad for voice lessons in the local advertising mailer, the *Foothills Trader*. After much fussing, I decided to call. My unexpected regret had been so startling to me that I wanted to take action right away, and the ad seemed like a sign. I met the teacher, a focused but friendly man named

Stephen Crawford[64] in his studio, an extra room of a pretty little house surrounded by maple trees. Standing next to the brown upright Baldwin piano, I sang "Someone to Watch Over Me," the old George and Ira Gershwin standard, while Mr. Crawford played. After I finished, he paused, then asked very gently in his beautiful resonant voice, "Cindy, what is it that you are hoping to accomplish? You're not contemplating any sort of, um, professional career are you?"

I replied that I just wanted to be able to stand up at a party and not be embarrassed, and maybe have someone say, "That was nice."

He said, "Ah. Well. We can work with that. If you're willing to do the work."

As you can probably guess, I was terrible. (There are videos.) But I was committed, and Steve was a wonderful teacher. I kept taking lessons and kept trying new things and new techniques. The work was difficult for me, and I had horrible stage fright, where my knees shook, my voice quavered, and I felt sick to my stomach. I have no problem speaking to groups of five hundred or a thousand people, but one person listening to me sing was a different matter. However, I wanted to sing and believed singing would enliven my life. And it has. Many years later, I now sing on a small-scale professional level, and while my stage fright is rarely gone completely, I am now told that I light up the stage. I learned that I can look, act and feel like a charismatic person, singing or speaking.

So light up your own stage. Do the work. Use the techniques from the nine charisma leverage areas you have read about and practiced to fully channel your power and enliven your career and your life. You have learned about connection and alignment and the way your natural wiring helps the free flow of your charismatic energy through you and out into the world. Throughout these pages you have learned that the simple secret to being charismatic is nothing more than using nine powerful levers to look, act and feel like a charismatic person. While it may take practice to bring those techniques into muscle memory and full usability, every step you have taken and every tip you have tried has increased your ability to have a positive impact and feel more deeply how your own charisma power flows within and through you. Let it grow, and become the inspirational leader who helps those around you succeed.

When I was preparing that first speech in 2009 that I mentioned way back in the introduction to this book, my mother asked me what I'd be speaking about. The speech didn't have a formal title at the time, but I told her I would talk about "executive presence." She looked surprised for a moment, paused, and then said, "That's great dear. I know most executives make a lot of money, but I suppose everyone likes presents."

I've kept that thought ever since.

In the beginning of the book I said that charisma is not about pretending to be someone else. Charisma is about having the discipline, focus and awareness to allow a clear path to the best you that you can be so that you can let your own true character come forward. Be the gift of your best self to the people around you.

Find your master switch. Breathe, raise your posture, set an intention, tell your listeners the message, make eye contact, and turn on your charisma. Light up your life and the lives of the people around you. As the famous American philosopher William James once said, "Act as if what you do makes a difference. It does."[65]

And stand up straight. Your mother was right.

APPENDIX 1

THE POWER OF YOUR BRAIN

(This article is an expanded version of the Day One readings.)

Your brain loops in repetitive thoughts that won't be still. Your hands shake when you know there's absolutely no reason to be nervous. You fall in love at first sight. You don't do any of these things on purpose, so then who or what is choosing to do those things?

Do you ever ask yourself who's in charge?

The simple answer is that you are, but only if anyone is. But who is this "you"? In order to reach your power switch and allow your charisma to flow freely you may find it helpful to broaden and understand your definition of who you are within your own body and brain.

A Management Issue

When I was growing up in East County, San Diego, I learned to ride from the father of a friend of mine on one of their horses, Ginger. Ginger was normally a sweet and obedient mare, but sometimes she would get something called "barn fever." If you've ever encountered that, you know what it feels like. The horse decides that now is the time to go home, back to the barn, and is pretty much unstoppable, especially by a young girl outweighed by some eight hundred pounds. When I complained about being unable to control Ginger, my friend's dad told me this: "Cindy," he said, "Never make the mistake of thinking that you really control any horse. The best you can hope for is to trick them into believing you're in charge."

Humans have a similar delusion about their own body and the higher intellect. We believe the conscious, thinking self is more or less in control of the body (at least the voluntary parts) rather than simply being a smart overseer that works somewhat imperfectly to manage things. In actuality, both the rider and the thinking conscious self are empowered only because the horse in one case, and the body in the other, has partially ceded control. Many times, the body becomes like a runaway horse, taking the bit in its mouth and speeding on dangerous ground, heading for home no matter how hard you pull back on the reins.

In order to understand why your body sometimes seems to be out of your control, it is useful to examine how your brain manages or doesn't manage things.

Three Parts of the Brain

First of all, you are marvelously made. What may appear to you to be unexpected or unrestrained responses are often part of your amazing complex system of back-up and redundancy, layered in your brain from the most primitive parts you have in common with most creatures, out to that phenomenal thin layer of gray whose complexity differentiates you from any other species on earth.

Simply put, the brain has three major areas: the brain stem, the limbic system and the cerebral cortex. Your brain stem sits on top of your spinal cord, your limbic system sits on top of the brain stem, and your cerebral cortex, also known as gray matter, wraps around most of the rest of the brain. The functions of the brain stem, limbic system and cerebral cortex are likewise stacked more-or-less in order, from the most elementary and primitive to the most complex and intellectual, and from the quickest and earliest receiver/processor of information to the last receiver/processor.

Imagine this visually by making a fist of your left hand. Your spinal chord is like your arm, your brain stem like your wrist, and the limbic system like your fist. Wrap your right hand around your left fist, and that is like your cerebral cortex.

The Brain Stem

The brain stem manages the most basic of functions, and you have this in common with pretty much any living thing with a spinal cord. The brain stem sits on top of the spinal cord and is your brain's first processor/receiver of information. Your brain stem does three key things:

Key life functions: The brain stem controls the key functions of life, including your breathing, heartbeat, level of alertness or arousal and other autonomic functions, like digestion.

Information from sensory nerves: The brain stem receives information from your sensory nerves and spinal cord.

Passes information to limbic system: The brain stem passes the sensory data up to the limbic system for further processing.

Your brain stem is step 1 for any sensory information or data coming into your brain. The information from the sensory nerves is received almost instantaneously by the brain stem and is passed to the limbic system a few hundredths of a second later.

The Limbic System

The limbic system is more of a convenient conceptual construct than an actual place. The limbic system refers to the group of organs generally placed on top of the brain stem. It is the step 2 receiver/processor of information in your brain. This system is generally more recently evolved and includes brain areas with roughly four sets of functions, mostly related to emotional processing and memory, and mostly above automatic reflex level but below conscious thought.

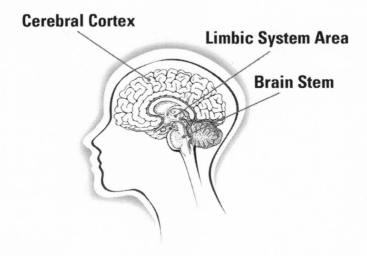

Smell/sensory perceptions: The limbic system processes your sense of smell (which is believed to be the earliest evolved of the traditional five senses), some other sensory perceptions and some basic movement functions.[66]

Emotional responses: The limbic system controls and interprets your emotional responses and drives, especially those related to survival instincts like hunger, fear, pleasure and sex, and regulates your hormones.

Sorts for memory: The limbic system decides what is noticed and what is remembered by selecting which information is sent to your hippocampus, the seat of long-term memory creation.

Sorts for importance: The limbic system also sorts information and tags it for emotional content. It judges incoming sensory data as safe or dangerous, good or bad, significant or irrelevant, and it filters what is sent on to the higher centers of your brain. Your core assumptions about the world that you believe to be true without thinking may be located here.

The noticing, remembering, and sorting that the limbic system does are particularly critical as you learn where your power really lies because these elements outline the way the limbic system filters the information before sending it on to your cerebral cortex. Note that all information must pass through the limbic system before you can process it intellectually at step 3, the cerebral cortex.

The Cerebral Cortex

The cerebral cortex is your "gray matter." It is that thin, wrinkly gray layer that encases most of the rest of your brain. It is your most recently evolved brain system and contains your higher intellectual system, the "thinking" part of the brain, and receives and processes information last, after it has passed through the brain stem and the limbic system. The cerebral cortex is the part of your brain that has the two hemispheres, right and left, you may have read about. Its main functions are:

Interprets sensory data: The cerebral cortex creates context and understanding, and makes sense of data. It tells you what things are.

Time, language, calculations: It makes complex, time-driven, planful decisions, uses language and numbers, and calculates.

Predicts: It sorts options, and guesses at potential outcomes.

Memory: It's involved with long-term and short-term memory and emotions.

The House of You

Think of the three-part brain as the electrical system of your house.

The brain stem is like the main power line coming into the house. Just as the line brings in electricity from the power grid, your brain stem brings in information from the world at large.

Like a power line, it doesn't bring in everything, just what is perceivable by your senses.

The limbic system is like the junction box on the side of your house. Just as your house's electrical system has a junction box with various fuses, circuit breakers and amperage-gauging systems that both direct and manage the safe flow of electricity, the limbic system both sorts information and acts as a safeguard.

The areas of your cerebral cortex are like all the appliances you turn on and off voluntarily within your house: lights, microwave, or computer. Your cortex manages how at least some of the information is used for language, calculating, predicting, and the rest of your conscious thinking.

You may think that the intellectual and conscious "you" is in control, at least mostly. However, just as no lights can be turned on without the electricity passing through the junction box of your house, the junction box of the limbic system controls much of what happens well before you have a chance to think consciously. This is important, and has two major aspects. First, the sorting and filtering function of the limbic system predisposes you to think in certain ways. Also, the safeguarding function of the limbic system acts as a protective circuit breaker to put you in action before you have time to make an intellectual decision.

The Limbic System Filters Everything

The limbic system gets all sensory information first. It processes every bit—repeat, every bit—of sensory data that comes from your body before it passes into your cerebral cortex. In the limbic system all data is evaluated, weighted and filtered for importance and given an emotional spin based on your deeply held core values about what you believe to be good/bad, dangerous/safe, worth noticing/not worth noticing or memorable/forgettable. Your core values are wired in to this older, preconscious emotional part of the brain and they create a set of default settings or shortcuts for a specific reaction. Some of those default settings, such as fear of falling, appear to be hardwired in,[67] others are developed over the course of living. Still others, such as the fear of spiders and snakes, appear to be somewhere in between, as if we are wired to develop a phobia of those things more easily than other objects.[68] The limbic system uses your core value system to pre-sort and pre-code every single piece of information with an emotion-driven tag based on those defaults. This means that your intellect is strongly predisposed to a specific reaction. Some information even gets preferential treatment. For example, your limbic center favors information that is deemed significant for immediate survival or that confirms prior evaluations.

When data does reach your higher cortex for evaluation and decision-making, it comes with judgments already put on it. Your attitude about any information you can think about has been created or heavily influenced preconsciously, based on your previous life experiences and your original wiring. It is interesting to note that your wired-in core values may differ from what you know or think you believe intellectually. You may know intellectually that flying is safe, but deep in your limbic system your fear of falling still exists. You may believe in your head and heart that all people are equal, yet apparently humans have a hard-wired core belief that people who look different are to be distrusted.[69] You can override these settings, but often only after your body has already reacted and generally with effort. Focus is required to pay attention and notice when your reactions are out of line with your conscious beliefs. If you keep choosing your intellectual beliefs long enough, you may convince your old limbic system and create a new paradigm for yourself.

Ancient Quick-Response Defense System

The second major aspect of the limbic system processing is its safeguarding or circuit breaker function, which relates to speed of response.

A beer bottle, knocked over on the kitchen counter, rolls off the edge. Your hand, somehow of its own volition, shoots out and catches the bottle before it drops to the floor. How did you do that? How many times have you amazed yourself by catching or deflecting something, or ducking a thrown object before you had any idea what had happened? Your friends say, "Wow—nice catch!" as the beer is saved from crashing on the tile. But who should get the credit? Did you make a conscious decision? Did you say to yourself, "Hmm, let me think about that... Should I catch that? What are the pros and cons of catching it? I believe I'll catch it now."

Of course you didn't. You catch the object reflexively, without thinking. This is part of your ancient quick-response defense system seated in your limbic system. Driven by fear, danger or biological need, the defense system is hard-wired into the preconscious older parts of the brain that have historically protected the body from immediate physical danger.

The journey of information from brain stem to limbic system to cerebral cortex to conscious decision and action can take two, or even up to three seconds. This delay is fine when there is time to plan, ponder, predict and deliberate, which is something the human cerebral cortex does very well. However, as impressive as your cerebral cortex and intellect are, there is an evolutionary advantage to the ability to have at least some automatic reactions to danger or opportunity without having to process information in the intellect, think and make a decision and delay by two or three seconds. Count out this time period to yourself. (One-potato, two-potato, three-potato.) In a primitive world, and even in a modern one, there are many things that can kill you in that period of time.

Speed matters. Just like you catching the rolling bottle, if your ancestors had relied on conscious thinking about their reactions to imminent threat, they'd never have survived to be your forebears. Think about a flock of birds that hears a noise, or a herd of antelope smelling a lion, or a horse that senses a snake. It doesn't take them two or three seconds to go to movement when a threat is perceived. The birds fly, the antelope run, the horse leaps away nearly instantaneously. What is true for them is true for you. Those primitive responses are still built into you.

That's where the circuit breaker function of the limbic system comes in. If your limbic system judges incoming sensory data to be dangerous or otherwise emotionally compelling, instead of simply tagging the information emotionally and passing it along to your intellect, the limbic system immediately sends messages back to the body controls in your brain stem, and causes your to body react without conscious thought, like a blown fuse or circuit breaker that doesn't allow overload current to pass. Just as the circuit breakers flip in your house automatically, your limbic system protects you and acts as a backup. The limbic system doesn't wait for instructions from your planful cerebral cortex, and may leave "you," the part you think of as your "self," temporarily out of the loop. The nearly instantaneous backward loop of your limbic system directly to your body saves valuable seconds.

This ancient defense system allows you to do things in a way that appears reflexive or automatic to your intellectual centers, like catching the falling beer bottle or ducking or pulling your hand back from a burning stove. You start to run or dodge before you specifically identify that large fast-moving object as a saber tooth tiger, falling boulder or New York City taxicab. This defense system also begins to power up the fight-or-flight adrenalized danger reactions you have no doubt heard of, which are more currently called fight-flight-or-freeze.[70] (Nice to know we have an additional choice.) Your limbic system makes your body jump, and simultaneously begins to prep your body for further fighting or flighting (or freezing) before the conscious you has time to think. Two to three seconds later, the conscious you may process the information and realize, "Oh—tiger/rock/cab" but only after you've already dodged, jumped, or started to run, and only after your body is filled with protection hormones, sending your heart and breathing rate up, and making you faster, stronger and more likely to escape. Conscious you in your newer cerebral cortex then survives to have the time to reflect and consider your actions, and busies itself figuring out cause and effect to try to keep you out of trouble in the future. There is logic to the idea of "jump first, think later."

The problem is your intellectual mind generally gives credence to what the body's reactions tell it. If your body is running, your intellect assumes there must be a good reason, at least initially. Your body's responses often tell your higher mind what to feel and how to react well before you are able to make any logical or intellectual calculations at all. This, combined with the fact that your limbic system has already pre-coded data as important/ unimportant and so on means that if you are not careful and attentive, your body and the emotional responses from your limbic system will commandeer your thinking. Sometimes the intellect doesn't even question the response, and may in fact rationalize it, as in "I was afraid of that guy because he was obviously dangerous," when rational thought might suggest an undue presumption of guilt.

Also, your limbic system is extremely stubborn in its desire to protect you, and will keep giving messages to reinforce those rationalizations. When your conscious cerebral cortex tries to overrule it by forcing you into what your limbic system has already decided is a dangerous situation, such as a battle, a fire, a speech to Wall Street investors, or singing solo at church, your limbic system speaks up and tells you over and over why you should run, typically warning you in the words and voice of a scolding, persistent, worried five-year-old. That voice is always on guard, ready to trip the circuits or ring the alarm bell, and it always seeks safety first. The voice may not be very smart, and may not always be right in a larger sense, but it saved your ancestors and allowed you to be born. In its sometimes simplistic way, it has your best interests at heart and could still save your life.[71]

The bottom line is this: In more cases than you generally notice, your body jumps first, and then your conscious mind considers. And, if your limbic system doesn't like your conscious mind's decision, it will nag you incessantly. It is extremely difficult for your intellect to talk your limbic system into or out of anything. However, your limbic system will listen to your body. So the trick is, as ever, to use your intellect to direct your body to go forward anyway, in a way that is powerful, upright and charismatic. Eventually, your limbic system will learn that you are safe.

APPENDIX 2

THE POWER OF YOUR EMPATHY: MIRROR NEURONS

(This article is an expanded version of the Day One readings.)

You may have heard it said, "No man is an island." This quote is from the writings of John Donne, the great English poet, priest and essayist.[72] This beautiful sentiment about the connection of everyone to each other turns out to be true from a neurological standpoint as well as a poetic one. You are connected at a measurable, preconscious level through a recently and accidentally discovered set of brain cells called "mirror neurons." Mirror neurons have been uncovered as the hard-wired biological basis for empathy. Your mirror neurons cause you to sync up with others, thus allowing you to understand what they are doing and make predictions about motives, intentions, and potential for danger and opportunity.

Here's a small example. This morning I was in my kitchen making coffee. From the bathroom down the hall, I heard the sound of my husband Paul's electric toothbrush. Immediately, I was more conscious of the taste of my own mouth and I could imagine the feel of the spinning brush head against my own teeth. Not only did I see Paul's actions in my mind's eye, in some way I felt those actions in my own body as well.

These feelings were mirror neurons at work. Mirror neurons help you by making you literally feel what others feel, react as they react, and imagine what it would be like to be in their shoes, on their island. Those feelings create or reinforce neural pathways, shift the vast array of connections in your brain and change who you are. These scientific findings about mirror neurons show us that other peoples' behaviors, actions and moods literally change you physically and neurologically. And you change other people in every single interaction you have. Through mirror neurons, you are in a constant state of co-creation of your attitudes, feelings and very self with the people around you.

Chemistry, vibes and gut reactions, mob and crowd behaviors[73] can be communication from this nonintellectual preconscious set of neurons. If you fail to recognize the messages from your mirror neurons, you will lose valuable information from the world around you and also risk confusing your own feelings with the feelings of others. Training yourself to recognize mirror neuron feedback more easily will make you more empathetic and more centered, both traits of a looking, acting and feeling like a charismatic and powerful leader.

A New Discovery

Scientists now understand how this happens in your brain. Twenty-odd years ago, in a neuroscience laboratory in Parma, Italy, a remarkable chance discovery was made.[74] Several macaque monkeys at the lab were being monitored using a new machine called an fMRI,[75] in an attempt to make a brain map of the monkey motor neurons for hand grasping. That is, the scientists were trying to determine where exactly in the brain the command and control center for the grasping function was located. The experimenters would give a monkey a cup, a piece of food, or some other object that required that the monkey reach out and grasp it. The scientists would then note where motor neurons fired in the monkey's brain.

One monkey was wired to the machinery but was not part of the active experiment at the time. It was simply waiting calmly in its chair, doing nothing in particular, when an experimenter noticed that the waiting monkey's motor neurons for grasping had fired, although the monkey itself hadn't moved a muscle. All it had done was observe one of the other monkeys picking something up.[76]

What the scientists discovered was that mirror neurons fire when you either observe or hear another creature performing an action. Someone brushes and you feel an almost physical sensation of the bristles against your own teeth, someone's hand grasps an ice cream cone and your own hand feels like it's grasping (and your mouth begins to water). The creature being observed doesn't have to be human. You just have to recognize the movement as translatable into your own imagination. A bird flying may make you feel like lifting your arms. Mirror neurons cause the circuitry in your brain to fire in a way that imitates, or mirrors, someone or something else's behaviors. Mirror neurons are different from other motor neurons because they do not cause your muscles to move, only to feel as if they had.

Mirror neurons help you process intention and make predictions about other creatures. You observe a movement in someone else, your mirror neurons mirror the behavior, and your preconscious processes how you would feel if you had made that same movement. For example, imagine that you see someone smile. Your mirror neurons for smiling fire, and for an instant your brain feels what it's like to smile. It says, "Oh, that's smiling I'm feeling. When I smile, it means I am happy, relaxed and pleased. Therefore, that other person is probably happy relaxed and pleased." You haven't smiled but feel almost as if you had. You make judgments about another's feelings based on how their actions make your own mirror neurons fire.

Think how happy or sad watching some behaviors make you. Seeing someone dance for joy makes you feel like dancing. Seeing someone cry makes your own face wrinkle in sympathy. Seeing your favorite team win a championship makes you feel as if you, yourself have played and won. Your mind, your psyche and your body are all affected. You don't do any of this consciously. You process the information deep in your brain with your mirror neurons, and only the empathetic conclusion rises to your surface consciousness.

Train Your Gut

You've no doubt heard someone say that a person, place or thing had good or bad vibes. You may have dismissed the idea as silly, but now you know vibes are not necessarily magical or mystical thinking. Vibes may be your mirror neurons picking something up that you have yet to bring to conscious awareness, which is coming through as a feeling or gut reaction. Since you now recognize that gut reactions and vibes may well have a legitimate source, you can train yourself to notice them more easily and pay attention.

Here's an exercise you can try. In the next week or so, be alert to physical sensations that come to you when you talk to others: weight, lightness, darkness, discomfort, pleasure and so on, especially when those sensations seem slightly disconnected from the words you are hearing. For example, someone might say, "It's a great project," but you feel your own stomach knotting up. Notice images that come to you in your mind's eye. Try to sense what comes from other peoples' reactions versus your own. Those images and feelings could be your mirror neurons throwing forward sensations, pictures and ideas to help you see intention, danger, opportunity or context. Those images and feelings may help you connect to the person you are speaking with.

I am told I am very intuitive. (Family tradition calls it "the Welsh blood.") However, I believe it is merely that I am in the habit of paying attention to what my body sensations and mind's eye are telling me and letting the information pass unjudged into my intellect rather than brushing it aside. I have also become reasonably good at separating my own responses from those of others. For example, often when a client is about to discuss something difficult with me, I have a physical sense of a huge weight being loaded onto my back. If I say, "Wow, I feel as if someone just dumped a sack of cement on me," invariably the person will tell me about something they are struggling with. I am usually able to recognize when the cement falls on me that it is not my own burden but is metaphoric weight coming from my client through my mirror neurons. The same is true when I feel an unexpected lifting of my spirits, as if someone had brightened the lights in the room. Then I know the person I am with is thinking about something they love.

Also, I pay attention to pictures that flash through my mind. I tell my clients that I will pass along these visual pictures because sometimes they make no sense to me logically, but they end up making metaphoric sense to the person I am with. For example, with one client, I "saw" a mental image of searching under a bed for a lost key. With another, I saw a giant steel block sitting on an empty patio. With another client, it was a huge column of ants. To my own amazement, all these images did in fact make sense to the clients I was with and turned out to be relevant sources of conversation. When you meet a new person, pause for a moment, and see what your mind kicks forward. Notice what your body tells you: what physical sensations occur, what pictures you see. The more you do this, the more your own intuition will astonish you, and the more easily you will find yourself "tuning in" to others around you. Positive power is created through connection. The more you tune in, the more connected you will be.

Surround Yourself with Positive Influences

Mirror neurons should make it clear to you that the influences with which you surround yourself are vitally important. As you might expect with something processed preconsciously, sometimes it is hard to completely disentangle what is "yours" from what is "theirs." Is it your delight, or theirs? Your bag of cement or theirs? Your mirror neurons connect you empathetically to everyone around you. Some of the good and bad emotions of others rub off on you literally, physically, and possibly permanently.

Every time you notice, feel or learn something, the neuronal pathways in your brain are strengthened around the topic, predisposing you to notice, feel or learn the same kinds of things in the future. Your brain is programmed to give preferential treatment to what it already knows or expects and to miss what it doesn't know or expect. What you experience significantly affects how your brain strengthens or creates new neuron connections, changing the way you see, feel and analyze things in the future, for better or worse. Your mirror neurons don't make your muscles move, but they still help create and strengthen neuronal connections about people, places and things. "No man is an island," or child or woman, either, or even a monkey in an Italian laboratory. Surround yourself with negative people and influences, and you will become weaker and more negative. This is true not because of "vibes" but because your brain chemistry makes it so.

Surround yourself with people who encourage, support and delight you, and you will become stronger and happier. The good they bring will bleed into your own heart, your own mind and body, via your mirror neurons. In that way, they will help you co-create a more positive, healthy self, through the growth, stimulus and strengthening of the neurons of your brain. Then you can go out and spread the good vibes.

Which is a pretty powerful outcome from a little mirror, right?

APPENDIX 3

SOME FURTHER READING

Blakeslee, Sandra, and Matthew Blakeslee. *The Body Has A Mind of Its Own: How Body Maps in Your Brain Help You Do (Almost) Everything Better.* New York: Random House, 2007.

Brizendine, Louann. *The Female Brain.* New York: Broadway Books, 2006.

Doidge, Norman. *The Brain That Changes Itself: Stories of Personal Triumph from the Frontiers of Brain Science.* New York: Penguin Books, 2007.

Dozier, Kimberly. *Breathing the Fire: Fighting to Report—And Survive—The War in Iraq.* Des Moines: Meredith Books, 2008.

Edwards, Betty. *Drawing on the Right Side of the Brain: A Course in Enhancing Creativity and Artistic Confidence.* Los Angeles: J. P. Tarcher, 1979.

Goleman, Daniel. *Social Intelligence: The New Science of Human Relationships.* New York: Bantam Books, 2006.

Gregory, Richard L. (editor). *The Oxford Companion to the Mind.* Oxford: Oxford University Press, 1987.

Hawk, Cathy and Gary Hawk. *Creating the Rest of Your Life, An Atlas for Manifesting Success & Excellence in Life & Work.* Edmonds, WA: Brilliance Press: 2007. An updated and expanded edition of this book is due for publication Fall, 2011. Its new title: *Get Clarity: The Lights-On Guide to Manifesting Success in Life and Work.*

Iacoboni, Marco. *Mirroring People: The New Science of How We Connect With Others.* New York: Farrar, Straus and Giroux, 2008.

Joseph, Arthur Samuel. *Vocal Power: Harnessing the Power Within.* Encino: Vocal Awareness Institute, 2003.

Laney, Marti Olsen. *The Introvert Advantage: How to Thrive in an Extrovert World.* New York: Workman Publishing, 2002.

Levitan, Daniel J. *This Is Your Brain On Music: The Science of A Human Obsession.* New York: Plume, 2006.

Loehr, Jim. *The Power of Story: Rewrite Your Destiny in Business and in Life.* New York: Free Press, 2007.

Loehr, Jim and Tony Schwartz. *The Power of Full Engagement.* New York: Free Press, 2003.

Maurer, Robert. *The Kaizen Way: One Small Step Can Change Your Life.* New York: Workman Publishing, 2004.

Navarro, Joe. *Louder Than Words: Take Your Career from Average to Exceptional with the Hidden Power of Nonverbal Intelligence.* New York: HarperBusiness, 2010.

Pink, Daniel. *A Whole New Mind: Why Right-Brainers Will Rule the Future.* New York: Riverhead Books, 2005.

Ratey, John J. *A User's Guide to the Brain: Perception, Attention and the Four Theaters of the Brain.* New York: Vintage Books, 2002.

Rock, David. *Quiet Leadership: Six Steps to Transforming Performance at Work.* New York: Collins, 2006.

Rock, David. *Your Brain at Work: Strategies for Overcoming Distraction, Regaining Focus, and Working Smarter All Day Long.* New York: Harper Business, 2009.

Seligman, Martin E. P. *Authentic Happiness: Using the New Positive Psychology to Realize Your Potential for Lasting Fulfillment.* New York: Free Press, 2002.

Seligman, Martin E. P. *Learned Optimism.* New York: Alfred A. Knopf, 1991.

Seligman, Martin E.P. *What You Can Change and What You Can't: The Complete Guide to Successful Self-Improvement.* New York: Alfred A. Knopf, 1993.

Siegel, Daniel J. *The Mindful Brain: Reflection and Attunement in the Cultivation of Well-Being.* New York: W. W. Norton, 2007.

Taylor, Jill Bolte. *My Stroke of Insight: A Brain Scientist's Personal Journey.* New York: Viking, 2006.

Thaler, Richard H. and Cass R. Sunstein. *Nudge: Improving Decisions About Health, Wealth, and Happiness.* New York: Penguin Books, 2008.

Zander, Rosamund Stone and Benjamin Zander. *The Art of Possibility: Transforming Professional and Personal Life.* New York: Penguin Books, 2000.

And anything by Oliver Sacks, Marshall Goldsmith or Malcolm Gladwell.

APPENDIX 4

When my brother and sister and I were children, our mother would recite poetry to us. This was one of her favorites, and I was fascinated by the story of the night, love, jealousy, sacrifice and blood. It may have ruined me for life.

THE HIGHWAYMAN by Alfred Noyes

Part One

The wind was a torrent of darkness among the gusty trees,
The moon was a ghostly galleon tossed upon cloudy seas,
The road was a ribbon of moonlight over the purple moor,
And the highwayman came riding—
Riding—riding—
The highwayman came riding, up to the old inn-door.

He'd a French cocked hat on his forehead, a bunch of lace at his chin,
A coat of the claret velvet, and breeches of brown doeskin;
They fitted with never a wrinkle: his boots were up to the thigh!

And he rode with a jeweled twinkle,
His pistol butts a-twinkle,
His rapier hilt a-twinkle, under the jeweled sky.

Over the cobbles he clattered and clashed in the dark inn-yard,
And he tapped with his whip on the shutters, but all was locked
and barred;
He whistled a tune to the window, and who should be waiting
there
But the landlord's black-eyed daughter,
Bess, the landlord's daughter,
Plaiting a dark red love knot into her long black hair.

And dark in the dark old inn-yard a stable-wicket creaked
Where Tim the ostler listened; his face was white and peaked;
His eyes were hollows of madness, his hair like moldy hay,
But he loved the landlord's daughter,
The landlord's red-lipped daughter,
Dumb as a dog he listened, and he heard the robber say—

"One kiss, my bonny sweetheart, I'm after a prize to-night,
But I shall be back with the yellow gold before the morning light;
Yet, if they press me sharply, and harry me through the day,
Then look for me by moonlight,
Watch for me by moonlight,
I'll come to thee by moonlight, though Hell should bar the way."

He rose upright in the stirrups; he scarce could reach her hand,
But she loosened her hair i' the casement! His face burnt like a
brand
As the black cascade of perfume came tumbling over his breast;
And he kissed its waves in the moonlight,
(Oh, sweet, black waves in the moonlight!)

Then he tugged at his rein in the moonlight, and galloped away
to the West.

Part Two

He did not come in the dawning; he did not come at noon;
And out o' the tawny sunset, before the rise o' the moon,
When the road was a gypsy's ribbon, looping the purple moor,
A red-coat troop came marching—
Marching—marching—
King George's men came marching, up to the old inn-door.

They said no word to the landlord, they drank his ale instead,
But they gagged his daughter and bound her to the foot of her
narrow bed;
Two of them knelt at her casement, with muskets at their side!
There was death at every window;
And hell at one dark window;
For Bess could see, through her casement, the road that he would
ride.

They had tied her up to attention, with many a sniggering jest;
They had bound a musket beside her, with the barrel beneath her
breast!
"Now, keep good watch!" and they kissed her.
  She heard the dead man say—
"Look for me by moonlight;
Watch for me by moonlight;
I'll come to thee by moonlight, though Hell should bar the way!"

She twisted her hands behind her; but all the knots held good!
She writhed her hands till her fingers were wet with sweat or
blood!

They stretched and strained in the darkness, and the hours
crawled by like years,
Till, now, on the stroke of midnight,
Cold, on the stroke of midnight,
The tip of one finger touched it! The trigger at least was hers!

The tip of one finger touched it; she strove no more for the rest!
Up, she stood up to attention, with the barrel beneath her breast,
She would not risk their hearing; she would not strive again;
For the road lay bare in the moonlight;
Blank and bare in the moonlight;
And the blood of her veins in the moonlight throbbed to her
love's refrain.

Tlot-tlot; tlot-tlot! Had they heard it? The horse-hoofs ringing
clear;
Tlot-tlot, tlot-tlot, in the distance? Were they deaf that they did
not hear?
Down the ribbon of moonlight, over the brow of the hill,
The highwayman came riding,
Riding, riding!
The red-coats looked to their priming! She stood up, straight and
still!

Tlot-tlot, in the frosty silence! Tlot-tlot, in the echoing night!
Nearer he came and nearer! Her face was like a light!
Her eyes grew wide for a moment; she drew one last deep breath,
Then her finger moved in the moonlight,
Her musket shattered the moonlight,
Shattered her breast in the moonlight and warned him— with
her death.

He turned; he spurred to the West; he did not know who stood

Bowed, with her head o'er the musket, drenched with her own red blood!

Not till the dawn he heard it, his face grew grey to hear

How Bess, the landlord's daughter,

The landlord's black-eyed daughter,

Had watched for her love in the moonlight, and died in the darkness there.

Back, he spurred like a madman, shrieking a curse to the sky,

With the white road smoking behind him and his rapier brandished high!

Blood-red were his spurs i' the golden noon; wine-red was his velvet coat,

When they shot him down on the highway,

Down like a dog on the highway,

And he lay in his blood on the highway, with the bunch of lace at his throat.

And still of a winter's night, they say, when the wind is in the trees,

When the moon is a ghostly galleon tossed upon cloudy seas,

When the road is a ribbon of moonlight over the purple moor,

A highwayman comes riding—

Riding—riding—

A highwayman comes riding, up to the old inn-door.

Over the cobbles he clatters and clangs in the dark inn-yard;

He taps with his whip on the shutters, but all is locked and barred;

He whistles a tune to the window, and who should be waiting there

But the landlord's black-eyed daughter,

Bess, the landlord's daughter,

Plaiting a dark red love knot into her long black hair.

NOTES AND SOURCES

1   The full text of Kimberly Dozier's post blog about the speech at: http://www.wowowow.com/post/body-language-standing-right-standing-wrong-kimberly-dozier-219586. In the speech, I only covered four or five of the 101 tips in this book. Ms. Dozier herself is an amazing and charismatic woman, a reporter who survived critical injuries from a 2006 car bomb attack in Bagdad that killed four of her team members. That year, she wrote an inspiring book about her recovery, *Breathing the Fire: Fighting to Report—And Survive—The War in Iraq.* Des Moines: Meredith Books, 2008.

2   Appendix I contains an expanded article on this topic. Also, see: Goleman, Daniel. *Social Intelligence: The New Science of Human Relationships,* New York: Bantam Books, 2006. And: Iacoboni, Marco. *Mirroring People: The New Science of How We Connect With Others.* New York: Farrar, Straus and Giroux, 2008.

3   Quoted by Andrew Burnham in a discussion on addiction, attributed to Eckman, David. *Sex, Food, and God: Breaking Free of*

Temptations, Compulsions and Addictions. Harvest House Publishers, September, 2006.

4   See, Ratey, John J. *A User's Guide to the Brain: Perception, Attention and the Four Theaters of the Brain.* New York: Vintage Books, 2002. Also, Gregory, Richard L. (editor). *The Oxford Companion to the Mind.* Oxford: Oxford University Press, 1987. For example (page 121), Ratey says, "The amygdala provides a preconscious bias of intensity to every stimulus you come into contact with, even before you can pay attention to it." There is also more information about the brain in Appendices 1 and 2.

5   Quoted in: Lambert, Craig. "The Psyche on Automatic." *Harvard Magazine,* November/December, 2010, http://harvardmagazine.com/2010/11/the-psyche-on-automatic.

6   John Donne, Meditation XVII from *Devotions Upon Emergent Occasions,* 1624. In part: "No man is an Island, entire of itself; every man is a piece of the Continent, a part of the main; if a clod be washed away by the sea, Europe is the less, as well as if a promontory were, as well as if a manor of thy friends or of thine own were; any man's death diminishes me, because I am involved in Mankind; And therefore never send to know for whom the bell tolls; It tolls for thee."

7   The original research that discovered mirror neurons discussed in this section and at greater length in Appendix 2, was done using macaque monkeys. See, Iacoboni, Marco. *Mirroring People: The New Science of How We Connect With Others.* New York: Farrar, Straus and Giroux, 2008, and Goleman, Daniel: *Social Intelligence, The New Science of Human Relationships,* New York: Bantam Books, 2006. There is also recent speculation that deficits in mirror neurons may possibly come into play in at least some parts of the autism spectrum.

8   Sandra Blakeslee and Matthew Blakeslee quoting psychologist Patricia Greenfield: "Other animals — monkeys, probably apes and possibly elephants, dolphins and dogs — have rudimentary mirror neurons, several mirror neuron experts

said. But humans, with their huge working memory, carry out far more sophisticated imitations." The Blakeslees further conjecture about dogs and mirror neurons in their book: Blakeslee, Sandra and Matthew Blakeslee. *The Body Has A Mind of Its Own: How Body Maps in Your Brain Help You Do (Almost) Everything Better.* New York: Random House Trade Paperbacks, 2007, 167.

9   An expanded article on mirror neurons is in Appendix 2.

10   Living cells do produce a bioelectric field. Bioelectrical signals are both created and detected in our cells, and passed through the nerve cells throughout our bodies.

11   Helen is still teaching in New York. www.helenbaldassare. com.

12   Morihei Ueshiba, martial artist and founder of the martial arts school of Aikido (1883-1969).

13   Abraham Lincoln, U.S. President (1861–1865).

14   Gracie Mansion is a beautiful old Federal-style mansion on the Upper East Side of Manhattan. Built in 1799, it is the official mayor's residence, and is also used for meetings, press conferences and other events.

15   See the Appendix I for a discussion of the limbic system.

16   "Sitz" is the correct spelling, from the German "sitzen," to sit.

17   From the Sanskrit "asan" meaning "body position."

18   Euripedes, ancient Greek tragic poet and playwright (ca 480 B.C.–406 B.C.).

19   Frank Zappa, American musician, film director and record producer (1940–1993).

20   A five-hundred-store chain formerly based in L.A., now morphed and subsumed into another iteration, mostly Rite-Aid, as I understand.

21   For those interested in seeing some of her art, Phebe Burnham's on-line gallery of works can be found at www.oldgraymare.net.

22 *Dress for Success*, by John T. Molloy, was published in 1975, and was the handbook for corporate attire for many years.

23 Data reported by the Gallup organization to account in part for the lack of women at the senior levels of U.S. corporations, in a speech by Jane Hart, associate partner, at the Executive Next Practices Forum, given December 2, 2010, in Irvine, CA.

24 F. Scott Fitzgerald, American writer and novelist (1896–1940).

25 Robert Brault, American freelance writer and consultant, see www.robertbrault.com.

26 Tweedledum and Tweedledee, two characters best known from Lewis Carroll's *Through the Looking Glass, and What Alice Saw There*. These twin brothers are round, like beach balls with legs and arms. They also have bad posture.

27 An excellent book on body language is Joe Navarro's *Louder Than Words: Take Your Career from Average to Exceptional with the Hidden Power of Nonverbal Intelligence*. New York: HarperBusiness, 2010.

28 Helen Keller, American author, activist, lecturer and advocate for people with disabilities (1880–1968).

29 Chaplin, William F.; Phillips, Jeffrey B.; Brown, Jonathan D.; Clanton, Nancy R.; and Stein, Jennifer L. "Handshaking, Gender, Personality and First Impressions." *Journal of Personality and Social Psychology*, 2000, Vol. 79, No. 1, 110-117.

30 Stewart, Greg L.; Dustin, Susan L.; Barrick, Murry R.; Darnold, Todd C. "Exploring the Handshake in Employment Interviews." *Journal of Applied Psychology*, Vol 98(5), Sept. 2008, 1139-1146.

31 No disrespect meant to the real Queen of England. I have no actual experience with her handshake, this is more by way of an imagined caricature.

32 Arvo Pärt, Estonian classical composer (1935–).

33 Benjamin Disraeli, British statesman (1804–1881).

34 I myself have used many coaches and teachers in vocal technique over the years, including Stephen Crawford, Nancy Stokes-Milnes, Helen Baldassare, Claude Stein, and currently Arthur Samuel Joseph and his partner Elizabeth Harmetz.

35 I highly recommend Arthur Samuel Joseph's book: *Vocal Power: Harnessing the Power Within*. Encino: Vocal Awareness Institute, 2003.

36 I am indebted to Arthur Samuel Joseph, Vocal Coach and founder of Vocal Awareness for the original idea that sparked this exercise.

37 May Sarton, American poet (1912–1995).

38 Ann Landers, pen name of American advice columnist. The source of this quote did not identify the date. The two main "Ann Landers" were Ruth Crowley, from 1943–1955, and Esther "Eppie" Lederer from 1955–2002. Several other authors also wrote under this name at different times.

39 Mark Twain, American humorist, lecturer and writer, pen name of Samuel Clemens (1835 – 1910).

40 This expression is from my good friend and editor, Henry DeVries.

41 Napoleon Hill, American author, speaker and success researcher (1883–1970).

42 Pearl Strachan Hurd, poet and staff writer for the Christian Science Monitor in the 1930s and later.

43 Dr. Robert N. Burnham, American educator and father (1920–1980).

44 Miller, B. (2010). The Effects of Scandalous Information on Recall of Policy-Related Information. *Political Psychology*, *31* (6), 887-914.

45 This quote is often attributed to Mark Twain. However, Twain apparently thought he was quoting Benjamin Disraeli, but was possibly quoting a man named Sir Charles Wentworth Dilke.

46 From the website of a lesion identifying technology company.

47   Technology such as the fMRI (functional magnetic imaging) machinery has shown this number to be incorrect. Even if it were correct, common sense should refute the relevancy of the number. The brain is like the rest of the body. Just because an organ or a muscle is not being used all the time does not mean it has extra capacity. Even your heart has spaces between beats. Just because your arm only moves a percentage of the time doesn't mean it gives capacity to your foot.

48   Lao Tzu, ancient Chinese mystical philosopher, author of the Tao Te Ching. Believed to have lived either in the sixth or fourth century B.C., and possibly mythical or the compilation of several historical figures.

49   Bruce Barton, American advertising executive and congressman (1886–1967).

50   Sir Winston Churchill, British statesman (1874–1965).

51   Some information about Paul Nichols and his music can be found at www.myspace.com/paulnicholsmusic.

52   See, Seligman, Martin E. P. *What You Can Change and What You Can't: The Complete Guide to Self-Improvement.* New York: Alfred A. Knopf, 1993.

53   In addition to all the tips that follow, go back to Week One: Charismatic Posture. Mastering the powerful positions given in that section trains your body to give powerful messages to your brain.

54   I learned a great deal about the monkey mind and other topics from Cathy and Gary Hawk, during a Clarity Workshop in January, 2007, and a number of Clarity Circle/Group Coaching sessions. Their book is an excellent source of guidance in uncovering and understanding one's life purpose. (*Creating the Rest of Your Life, An Atlas for Manifesting Success & Excellence in Life & Work.* Edmonds, WA: Brilliance Press: 2007.) The topic of monkey mind is discussed extensively on pages 93-96, and 103-105. An updated and expanded edition of their book is due to be released Fall, 2011. Its new title

is: *Get Clarity: The Lights-On Guide to Manifesting Success in Life and Work.* www.getclarity.com

55 Another kind of meditative activity is to be involved in something that requires your total attention. For me, that is singing in a choir or playing music where I have to sight-sing or sight-read. I guarantee that sight-singing and worrying about the past or future are pretty much incompatible. This may also be part of golf's appeal for many people.

56 Quoted in: Lambert, Craig, "The Psyche on Automatic," *Harvard Magazine* (November/December, 2010): http://harvardmagazine.com/2010/11/the-psyche-on-automatic

57 Indian political leader and philosopher, Mohandas, a.k.a. Mahatma ("Great Soul") Gandhi (1869–1948).

58 Abraham Lincoln, American president and statesman (1809–1865).

59 A wonderful book on this topic is by Jim Loehr: *The Power of Story: Rewrite Your Destiny in Business and in Life.* New York: Free Press, 2007. Also, Martin Seligman discusses the importance of positive inner dialog in his groundbreaking book, *Learned Optimism,* first published by Alfred A. Knopf, New York, in 1991. *Learned Optimism* is one of the origins of the Positive Psychology movement, and is still in print.

60 See, Joseph, Arthur Samuel. *Vocal Power: Harnessing the Power Within.* Encino: Vocal Awareness Institute, 2003, 36.

61 Liz Goodgold, author of *RED FIRE BRANDING: Create a Hot Personal Brand and Have Customers for Life* and *DUH! Marketing.*

62 See Appendix 2 for an expanded discussion of mirror neurons and your empathy circuitry.

63 Taylor, Jill Bolte. *My Stroke of Insight: A Brain Scientist's Personal Journey.* New York: Viking, 2006, 172.

64 Stephen Crawford still teaches and has a great performance school in Phoenix (www.thespiritedheart.com).

65 William James, American philosopher, psychologist, writer, and educator (1842–1910).

66   The sense of smell (See, Ratey, John, *A User's Guide to the Brain*) is the only sense that doesn't go through the brain stem but goes direct to the amygdala in the limbic system. Reactions to smell are faster, more directly emotional, and less "mediated" by other areas of the brain than the other senses.

67   Gibson, E. J., and Walk, R. D. (1960). "The Visual Cliff." *Scientific American*, 202, 67–71. Babies of a certain developmental age avoid crossing a bridge where an optical illusion makes it appear to be a cliff.

68   These are called "evolutionarily prepared" objects. Martin Seligman, in a discussion of this topic says, "Some of what we are – our darkest fears, for example – originated early in the evolution of our species. (Seligman, Martin E.P. *What You Can Change and What You Can't*. 82-83.)

69   Ibid.

70   New thinking also suggests that women have an additional or related reaction of "tend-and-befriend," which may be why, in my very casual non-scientific noticing, women tend to be more likely to hug, or grab someone else's hand during threatening or scary moments.

71   Cathy Hawk and Gary Hawk. Ibid., plus other brain articles and lectures.

72   John Donne, Ibid.

73   Mirror neurons may also explain synchronized swimming, if that is explainable.

74   I have heard this story reported in a variety of books and articles. Two good ones are: Goleman, Daniel. *Social Intelligence: The New Science of Human Relationships.* New York: Bantam Books, 2006, and Iacoboni, Marco. *Mirroring People: The New Science of How We Connect With Others.* New York: Farrar, Straus and Giroux, 2008.

75   fMRI, or Functional MRI, stands for "functional magnetic resonance imaging." fMRI machines can measure changes in blood flow in the brain while the changes are occurring, or

functioning. The original MRI machines were more typically used to look at static tissue images for pictures to do things like locate damage or tumors. The new machinery is more focused on activities and how they occur. The fMRI machine is so sensitive it can discern the location and firing of a single neuron.

76 I have also read it reported that it may have been a person being observed, either using a cup or eating an ice cream cone, or perhaps a raisin was involved. Whatever was grasped and by whom, the resultant discovery was the same.

Made in the USA
Charleston, SC
14 March 2012